Law in Sport

Liability Cases in
Management and
Administration

Bernard Patrick Maloy, J.D., M.SA.

LAW IN SPORT: LIABILITY CASES IN MANAGEMENT AND ADMINISTRATION

BERNARD PATRICK MALOY, J.D., M.SA.
UNIVERSITY OF MICHIGAN

Benchmark Press, Inc.
Indianapolis, Indiana

Library of Congress Cataloging in Publication Data:

Maloy, Bernard Patrick 1947-

Law In Sport: Liability Cases in Management and Administration

Cover Design: Gary Schmitt
Copy Editor: Lynn Hendershot

Library of Congress Catalog Card number: 88-70146

ISBN: 0-936157-30-5

Printed in the United States of America
10 9 8 7 6 5 4 3 2 1

Library of Congress Cataloging in Publication Data:

Maloy, Bernard Patrick 1947-

Law In Sport: Liability Cases in Management and Administration

Cover Design: Gary Schmitt
Copy Editor: Lynn Hendershot

Library of Congress Catalog Card number: 88-70146

ISBN: 0-936157-30-5

Printed in the United States of America
10 9 8 7 6 5 4 3 2 1

The Publisher and Author disclaim responsibility for any adverse effects or consequences from the misapplication or injudicious use of the information contained within this text.

Contents

Preface

The specific focus of this text is liability in the sports management function, not a broad application of legal aspects in sport. Notably, the book does not include material on the judicial process or civil procedure; there is very little I can add to those areas that has not adequately been covered by other texts. And, while an understanding of the court system may be interesting to the reader, a manager's ability to identify operational risks will be more beneficial.

The text is intended to teach the sports management student and aid the sports administrator by the selection of pertinent topics, by utilizing recent case law, and by emphasizing specific areas which impact on sports management.

The key to the book is the edited cases used to highlight significant managerial responsibilities. Case selection was not limited to judicially-completed cases. Many of the cases have been sent back to the trial court from appeal for a new trial or rehearing. The cases were selected on the basis of their unique facts and issues. The cases were to address the management process, not merely the final legal resolution. Finally, the case law was edited to serve as a practical road map for today's sports manager. Many times legal opinions contain issues or points of law that may not be important for the sports administrator. I have attempted to focus on the practical issues of management liability.

When I was selecting topics for the book, a question frequently asked was why I chose workmen's compensation as an appropriate subject for a sports management text. The answer is easy. Ask any organizational administrator about the impact of workmen's compensation on the organization's budgeting process, production schedules, compliance with health and safety regulations, or employee performance. My experience as an advocate, manager, and consultant for sports-related clients is that organizational managers and administrators find workmen's compensation and its processes just as important as the other administrative duties of their jobs.

I have provided a brief overview of workmen's compensation with an emphasis on work-related stress. Too often, workmen's compensation is understood solely in the context of industrial injuries, or as an insurance component of organizational budgeting. The judicial recognition of stress as a cause of work-related injuries affects all product or service industries. Therefore, today's sports adminstrator is advised that workmen's compensation is important for all industries, mot merely those whose employees may be threatened by industrial hazards. Employee motivation and expectation, which are related to stress, are scrutinized by the courts for their causal connection to work-related injuries.

In addition to workmen's compensation, today's sports administrator is required to provide services in a safe and secure facility, to use safe equipment, and to work with with regulatory agencies. Therefore, cases in facility management, immunity applications, physical education issues, athletic associations, and other athletic issues were included in the text.

This text contains cases reported from October, 1986 through December, 1987. Although they should capably supplement the other works in sports law, they are intended to serve as source material for the *law of sports management*.

There is another perspective to consider. Those who have studied case law realize that its value is not confined to legal precedent. Case law is as valuable a political, historical, or social report as any written tool in our society. Case law has proven to be a valuable teaching tool, and it provides a time-honored background for the administrator to learn from past lessons.

The sports environment is part of what is termed a "litigious society." However, I believe that phrase is inaccurate because it also implies that our society resolves its conflicts through the judicial system. In fact, we are a society that brings conflicts to the judicial system, but resolves the majority of them through negotiated settlement. Because many civil liability cases are settled out of court, we depend little on the reasoning of the judicial system for final resolution. Therefore, the sports administrator can learn from the judicial system, but he or she must rely on prudent *managerial skills* to capably perform the job.

In a society where conflict resolution is generally not decided by the judicial process, the efforts of many attorneys who represent administrative and managerial clients is best directed to insure the sports administrator has the best available information to incorporate as a management skill in his or her job.

I wish to thank Bernard F. Maloy of Chevy Chase, Maryland, for his guidance and counsel during this project; and, Mark and Marge Alton of Lillian, Alabama, whose support made it possible.

Pat Maloy

Chapter 1

Facility Management

INTRODUCTION

There are two benefits of studying tort liability in facility management: first, it provides a focus for specific areas of concern or interest to the facility operator; and second, facility liability is a valuable learning tool for the legal concepts of negligence, intentional misconduct, and dangerous conditions.

Facility management, a high visibility, people business, must concern itself with tort liability. Whether viewed from the legal liability standpoint, or from a successful marketing and management awareness, the safety measures provided for recreational and sports facility users should be of primary concern to the facility operator.

Tort liability is concerned with the manner in which the facility is maintained for the safety of its users. Safety procedures require that the facility operator understands who the users are; how to best utilize the staff experience for recognizing potential user dangers; how to react to unruly, volatile, or intoxicated patrons; how to allocate supervisory duties; and how to recognize unusual conditions that threaten the safety of children using the facility. Liability is legally measured by the reasonable or prudent efforts taken to secure user or patron safety. Of course, there are instances when facility users assume the risk of injury.

Traditionally, facility users, including house guests, have legally been categorized as "invitees" or "licensees." Each designation carried a corresponding degree of care owed by the property owner. There was a third category for trespassers on the property.[1] These categories have strong legal and historical roots. However, their interpretation and the requisite duties of conduct have changed through time.

Briefly stated, the traditional duties of the property owner were:

1. No duty of care was owed to trespassers since their entrance on the property was without the permission of the owner. Trespassers took the land as they found it since the owner was not required to warn of any dangerous conditions that may be encountered.

2. A licensee entered the property with the permission of the owner, however, only for a purpose suited for the benefit of the user. The duty of care owed to licensees was very limited, usually only a warning of known dangers.

3. An invitee entered the property with permission, or invitation, of the owner. The entry was for a purpose beneficial to the owner (generally, economic). The duty owed to an invitee was an affirmative duty, that is, the owner had to actively maintain the premises in reasonably safe condition; had to repair defects; and had to warn of known dangers, or dangers which could have been reasonably discovered.

Regarding the duties of care owed to facility users, it is important to realize that the legal classification of users has little meaning when a recreational facility operates for profit or has some other inherent, beneficial purpose to its operation.

However, there appears to be a new judicial effort to apply general rules of negligence to these issues, leaving the traditional classifications as but one of many circumstances to be considered by the court. Therefore, the facility owner must be aware of the judicial inconsistencies that may arise in the application of the categories.

HOW DO YOU TAKE CARE OF YOUR USERS

If a facility operator treats all users as invitees and assumes the affirmative care for their safety, the facility will have met the legal obligation of reasonable care regardless of the users' legal status. An interesting dilemma is presented by university recreational facilities. If classification rules are applied to student users, are those students owed a duty of affirmative care as "invitees," or the limited duty of care as "licensees?" Keep in mind, the classical distinction between the designations relates to who is getting the benefit from the use of the facility. In *Light v. Ohio University*, that question was easier to answer since the user, a member of the general public, was not charged a fee for her use of the facility.

A user who exercises at an Ohio University gymnasium, without charge, is a licensee and is owed a very limited duty of care.

LIGHT V. OHIO UNIVERSITY
502 N.E.2d 611
Supreme Court of Ohio
December 24, 1986

FACTS. A mother brought her five-year-old daughter with her to an exercise class at Grover Center gymnasium on the campus of Ohio University. The little girl was injured when a row of lockers fell on her, apparently as a result of her climbing or hanging onto them. The mother did not pay a fee to use the facility.

The Ohio Supreme Court rejected the mother's claim that she and her daughter were owed the duty of ordinary care. The court ruled they were "licensees," and the university only owed them the duty to refrain from wilful and wanton misconduct.

ISSUE. An *invitee* is a person who enters the premises of another by express or implied invitation, for a purpose that is beneficial to the owner of the premises. A *licensee* is a person who comes on the premises of another, without invitation, for his or her benefit.

DECISION. Ohio University had consented to allow the public to use its facilities, and had assumed the full costs of such use (except locker rental which was incidental, not a commercial venture). Based on that use, the plaintiffs were licensees to whom Ohio University only owed the duty to refrain from any wilful and wanton misconduct which could cause them harm.

Reasonable Care

A facility owes its users a duty to exercise reasonable care for their safety. Generally, the exercise of that care depends on the operator's knowledge of the risks or dangers confronting the user. Consider the precautions taken by Louisiana Downs to safeguard the property of its patrons in *Willis v. Louisiana Downs, Inc.*

A race track which charges parking fees owes the same duty of care to protect its patron's vehicles as it would its own property.

WILLIS V. LOUISIANA DOWNS, INC
499 So.2d 155
Court of Appeal of Louisiana, 2nd District
October 29, 1986

FACTS. The Oklahoma State University men's golf team was in Shreveport, Louisiana, to play in a tournament. Some team members, with the team coach and his wife, attended the races at Louisiana Downs racetrack. They paid a $1.00 fee to park the school van in the track parking lot. Golf clubs, jewelry, and a purse were stolen from the van while the team was at the track.

The court ruled in favor of Louisiana Downs when the team sued to recover for loss of the stolen items. The court ruled the race track had exercised due care protecting the parked vehicle and its contents.

ISSUE. What duty of care, if any, did Louisiana Downs owe to its patrons who paid to park?

DECISION. Louisiana Downs was a "compensated depository"; therefore, it was bound to use the same care that it would use to protect its own property. That responsibility extends to the van's component parts, including tires and wheels.

The same duty would extend to personal items left in the van if Louisiana Downs had expressly or impliedly consented to accept that responsibility. However, since the items were located on the floor of the van, underneath the seats, there were no circumstances to indicate that the defendant knew, or should have known, that valuables were in the van.

A compensated depository must exercise the ordinary care of a prudent person. If there is a loss, the law presumes the depository was negligent or at fault.

In this case, however, the defendant overcame that presumption by showing that 10 people were on surveillance duties, and an additional 20 employees were on parking duties. Also, there were marked and unmarked cars patrolling the parking lot, and surveillance from the grandstands as well as the parking lot. The evidence was sufficient to show the track had used due care to protect parked vehicles.

If the facility has breached its duty of care, the user must be able to prove a causal relationship between that breach and the user's resulting injury. For example, in *East Bay Raceway v. Parham*, there was a question of whether the faulty condition of a protective wall at an auto race track had a causal relationship to the injury of a spectator.

This race track is not liable to a spectator struck by an out-of-control, airborne race car.

EAST BAY RACEWAY V. PARHAM
497 So.2d 719
District Court of Appeal of Florida, 2nd District
November 12, 1986

FACTS. A spectator at East Bay Raceway (Florida) was standing behind a wall and gate adjacent to the auto race track. During a race, a race car collided with another car, hit a guard rail, "pole vaulted" over the protective wall and gate, and struck the spectator, causing severe injuries.

The spectator filed a lawsuit against the track claiming his injuries were the result of the poor condition of the protective wall and gate. The court disagreed and ruled that the spectator's injury was not caused by a faulty wall and that he failed to prove the race track deviated from a reasonable standard of care for his safety.

ISSUE. What duties of care did the race track owe to its spectators? Did this injury occur as a result of the faulty condition of the wall and gate which protects patrons from the race cars?

DECISION. The raceway has the duty to exercise reasonable care to its patrons. However,

> "In order to establish a breach of that duty, (plaintiff) had the burden of proving that (East Bay) had knowledge of a condition which caused the accident, that a reasonable race track owner would have exercised greater caution, and that there was a causal connnection between the incident causing injury and a negligent act by appellant (East Bay)." (p. 720)

The spectator failed to prove that East Bay deviated from a reasonable standard of care, how the alleged faulty construction of the wall caused his injuries, or how it could have prevented injury from an "airborne" vehicle.

Invitation and Area of Invitation

Is there a risk for the facility operator who assumes the facility only owes a limited duty of care when the primary use of the facility is for the user's benefit? In the case of a public facility, a facility which promotes student use, or a facility which encourages youth programs, the risk may be costly.

As noted, there is a trend to de-emphasize the impact of the user's legal status on a facility's potential liability. A facility which, expressly or implicitly, encourages its use may owe the affirmative duty of care, regardless of who receives the primary benefit. In Chapter Two,

"Immunity Applications," we see the courts struggling with the application of user status to injuries suffered in urban parks and pools. Many courts consider those facilities excluded from the protection of recreational use immunity since they implicitly encourage the use of their facilities by the general public.

Does an urban facility, whose use is encouraged and promoted to the general public, have the affirmative duty of care to its users? While the facility use may be beneficial to the user, logic demands that the court examine whether, in fact, the facility "invites" its use by the public. Obviously, the promotion, advertising, and other marketing strategies used by a recreational facility will have a major impact on that consideration. It should be assumed that a court would be hard pressed to base a liability decision solely on identifying who received the benefit if the use of the facility was encouraged or invited.

The concept of an implicit invitation by the facility should not be confused with "area of invitation." The area of invitation in *Codd v. Stevens Pass, Inc.* was defined as the area of a ski facility that must be maintained for skiers.

The "area of invitation" of a ski area is the entire area serviced by chair lifts, not merely the groomed trails.

CODD V. STEVENS PASS, INC.
725 P.2d 1008
Court of Appeals of Washington
Sept. 22, 1986

FACTS. The decedent and his teenage son chose to ski an "ungroomed" area between two "groomed" trails at the ski area operated by the defendant. The area had many moguls; the decedent fell during his run, struck his head on a mogul, and was killed.

The court granted his widow a new trial in her lawsuit against the defendant. The court ruled that the jury should consider whether or not the defendant had met the duties of care owed to the decedent.

ISSUE. What, if any, duties of care did the ski operator owe? Did the decedent assume the risk of injury?

DECISION. The decedent was an invitee at Stevens Pass, so the ski operator owed an affirmative duty to use reasonable care to repair dangerous conditions; to maintain the premises in reasonably safe condition; and to warn of any hazards, if known. The duty extended only to "the area of invitation," that is, where the invitee was "reasonably led to believe is open to him."

The ski operator's defense was a Washington statute which stated, in part:

> ". . . any person skiing on other than improved trails or slopes within the area shall be responsible for any injuries or losses resulting from his or her action." (p. 1011)

The operator argued that the ungroomed area was not an improved trail.

However, the area of invitation was determined to be that area served by the chair lift. In this case, improvement was not gauged by the grooming of a ski trail, but by the change from tow ropes to chair lifts which made the entire area more accessible to skiers. The ski operator had a duty to discover hazards in the entire area (including ungroomed trails) serviced by the chair lift and to repair them or warn the skiers of their danger.

THE FORESEEABILITY FACTOR

The exercise of reasonable or ordinary care is merely a legal definition. Its application is for the facility operator who can utilize his or her knowledge, past experience, and perception to recognize, and guard against potential liabilities.

The liability issues faced by most recreational facilities have one common theme: could it reasonably be expected or foreseen that the user would be injured by that particular risk or danger? Legal scholars debate the role of foreseeability as a causal factor to a user's injury or loss. But, the facililty operator only needs to know whether or not the risk of danger was one that could have been prevented. When liability results from foreseeable dangers, it usually means the facility operator has not prudently used his or her abilities (knowledge, experience, and perception).

Foreseeable Circumstances

Many times the foreseeable risks or dangers to the users are obvious, as in *Bishop V. Fair Lanes Georgis Bowling, Inc.*

A bowling alley's duty to maintain safe premises includes the duty to protect patrons from apparent and foreseeable assaults.

BISHOP V. FAIR LANES GEORGIA BOWLING, INC.
803 F.2d 1548
United States Court of Appeals, 11th Cir.
November 12, 1986

FACTS. The plaintiff and his companion attended "Midnight Madness" at the Fair Lanes bowling alley. The defendant and his group of companions were at the adjacent lane, visibly intoxicated. The two groups got into an argument over a missing pitcher of beer.

The plaintiff advised the management of the bowling alley that the defendant and his friends were drunk, making a commotion, and acting in a threatening and aggressive manner. The management watched the defendant and his group for a short period of time, but took no action. At closing, the plaintiff was assaulted and severely beaten by the defendant in the bowling alley's parking lot.

The plaintiff sued the defendant and Fair Lanes. After the trial court denied the plaintiff's claim, the court of appeals granted the plaintiff a new trial because there were genuine issues of fact regarding Fair Lanes's duty to the plaintiff which had not been decided by the trial court.

ISSUE. What duties of care were owed by Fair Lanes to the plaintiff?

DECISION. The law required that the bowling alley exercise reasonable care to maintain safe premises for its patrons. In Georgia, the law was even more strict since the duty was defined as "safe" premises, not just "reasonably safe" premises.

The issue here was the bowling alley's failure to protect the plaintiff from apparent and foreseeable dangers. The court ruled against the bowling alley because its management did not stop selling beer to the obviously intoxicated defendant and his group and had failed to prevent the assault despite two warnings by the plaintiff.

Unusual Circumstances

The degree or magnitude of the foreseeable risk can be diffcult to gauge.

This bowling alley could not reasonably foresee that an irate husband would attempt to shoot his estranged wife on its premises.

HADDOX V. SUBURBAN LANES
349 S.E.2d 910
Supreme Court of Appeals of West Virginia
October 28, 1986

FACTS. A husband and wife were experiencing marital problems. He had been arrested for disorderly conduct and intoxication at the bowling alley following an argument with his wife. Two weeks later, his wife refused to speak with him, while she was at the same bowling alley. However, she feared that he would attempt to bother her, so a policeman was called to escort her home. Before she could leave, her husband walked into the bowling alley unseen, drew a gun, and started shooting at his wife. An errant slug struck and injured the plaintiff.

The plaintiff sued the bowling alley for its negligence in allowing the husband, known as a violent and dangerous character, on its premises. The court rejected the claim, and ruled that the bowling alley was not negligent.

ISSUE. Suburban Lanes owed its patrons the duty to exercise ordinary care to keep and maintain the premises reasonably safe. Should the bowling alley have foreseen the danger posed by the irate husband?

DECISION. It might have been expected that the husband would start a disturbance, but no one expected he would attempt to shoot his wife. The police officer did not have a weapon; an acquaintance who had seen the husband in the parking lot prior to the shooting was not unduly fearful, and no action was taken by the officer to inform the bowling center employees of any danger.

Accordingly, Suburban Lanes was not liable for the plaintiff's injury since that injury could not have been reasonably anticipated, and would not have occurred without unusual circumstances.

A probable weakness in the *Haddox* decision was that the court did not impose a duty on the bowling alley to be aware of the husband's presence. The failure to make anyone aware of his presence was laid at the feet of the wife and the police officer, who failed to convey concerns to the management. Considering the recent attacks by the husband against his wife, it *could* be legitimately argued that the management had a duty to know who entered its premises.

Actual Knowledge

Obviously, a facility's knowledge of a risk of danger to its users is the key to measuring foreseeability. In many instances, the constructive knowledge of a risk or danger is sufficient to impose tort liability. Constructive knowledge is determined objectively by asking what the facility operator should have known, what care the facility operator should have taken to reasonably discover the risk or danger, and what would a reasonable person under similar circumstances have known.

Conversely, actual knowledge is determined by the subjective test that requires proof of what the owner actually knew. When the law requires actual knowledge of a risk or danger to measure foreseeability, it is difficult to challenge the facility for its failure to prevent the risk of injury to the patron or user.

Minnesota requires that its state parks have actual knowledge of dangers before liability will be imposed for injuries to campers.

HENRY V. STATE
406 N.W.2d 608
Court of Appeals of Minnesota
June 9, 1987

FACTS. A family camped at Helmer Myre State Park, part of the outdoor recreational system operated by the state of Minnesota. The park contained campfire rings, parking, toilets, showers, sewers, and electrical lines. The parents slept in one tent; their two children slept in a separate tent. During an early morning storm, the limb of a tree fell onto the children's tent, killing one child and permanently injuring the other.

The parents filed a lawsuit against the state of Minnesota alleging the park had been negligently maintained. The court dismissed their claim, ruling that Minnesota was protected by immunity.

ISSUE. Minnesota is immune from liability for injuries caused by *natural* conditions in its outdoor recreational system. However, it is not protected by immunity when it creates or maintains an artificial condition likely to cause death or maintains a dangerous condition without providing adequate warning.

The limb that fell on the children's tent was from a tree that was diseased and decayed. Is that a natural or an artificial condition?

DECISION. The plaintiffs were able to show that the tree's disease was a result of soil compaction from the development of the park; and, that a year before the accident, a similar storm had blown through the area causing damage to the trees. The court rejected their contention that these facts were evidence of an artificial condition, citing that an artificial condition is generally found only if there is some type of trap or concealment.

Further, it appeared that the state did not have actual knowledge of any condition for which the tree limb was likely to cause death or serious harm.

The court reasoned that the state had no duty to inspect for hidden dangers caused by natural conditions, therefore, it was unreasonable to require the state to have constructive knowledge, or "reason to know" of the danger or defect. There was strong dissent to this point since liability would be predicated on what the state knew, rather than what the state *should* know.

USER PROBLEMS

The facility operator often is responsible for the safety and care of the patrons. However, there are situations when a duty of care is not required; or, where the duty ends.

Alcohol

Intoxication is always a problem because of the supervision and safety problems it presents. In addition, facility operators should be concerned with the manner in which alcohol is procured, its use on the premises, and its effect on other users of the facility. Although a facility can eject an intoxicated patron, the duty of care to the patron may not end at the door.

Intoxicated patrons bear the responsibility for their own condition.

Rutgers University does not have the duty to protect its intoxicated football fans from their own drunkenness.

ALLEN V. RUTGERS, THE STATE UNIVERSITY OF NEW JERSEY
523 A.2d 262
Superior Court of New Jersey, Appellate Division
March 25, 1987

FACTS. An intoxicated Rutgers student, attending a football game at the university stadium, mistakenly jumped a four-foot wall onto steps 30 feet below. He suffered permanent injuries from the fall.

At the time of the fall, Rutgers prohibited the consumption of alcoholic beverages during games, checked packages and containers at entry to the stadium, and escorted intoxicated individuals from the stadium. In this case, the student and his friends entered the stadium with a multi-gallon container of alcoholic beverage, became progressively more intoxicated in full view of stadium personnel, and repeatedly had to be restrained from going onto the field. But, they were not ejected from the stadium.

The jury returned a verdict against the student's claim that Rutgers had breached an assumed duty to protect him from his own intoxication.

ISSUE. If a university prohibits the use of alcoholic beverages, checks containers and packages, and has a policy of escorting intoxicated individuals from its premises, does it assume a duty to protect those individuals? Does a university have a duty similar to a tavern owner, under dram shop laws, to protect patrons from their own intoxication?

DECISION. Dram shop laws impose on tavern owners the duty to refrain from serving intoxicants to visibly intoxicated patrons. However, that duty is not applicable to this case. Rutgers did not serve or sell alcoholic beverages; nor was there any reason to impose sole responsibility on the university for failing to effectively enforce their own rules when a patron voluntarily chooses to become intoxicated

The court also rejected the logic of the student's argument that the university owed a duty to protect him from his own "folly."

A skating rink owes no duty of care to intoxicated patrons who leave the premises in the care of friends.

DUMKA V. QUADERER
390 N.W.2d 200
Court of Appeals of Michigan
April 21, 1986

FACTS. Due to his intoxication, the decedent was ejected from the defendant's skating rink. His companion left him sleeping in a car, and returned to the rink. Later, the companion checked on the decedent, and found him barely conscious. When the companion returned to the car a second time, the decedent was gone. His body was found two days later, a victim of exposure to snow and cold.

The decedent's estate filed a lawsuit alleging the skating rink breached a duty to care for the decedent who was a paid patron. The court dismissed the case.

ISSUE. What duty, if any, was owed to the decedent? Is the rink liable for placing the decedent in greater peril by expelling him from the premises?

DECISION. The skating rink owed the decedent the duty to exercise ordinary and prudent care for his safety, and to maintain the rink in a reasonably safe manner. However, that duty ended when the decedent left the premises escorted by and in the care of a friend, regardless of the paid admission.

Because the decedent was placed in the care of the friend, the defendant was relieved of any further liability, including placing the decedent in a position of greater peril.

Supervision

The issue in *Dillon v. Keatington Racquetball Club* was whether a recreational facility had the duty to supervise all user activities on its premises.

Generally, a recreational facility does not have a duty to supervise informal games.

DILLON V. KEATINGTON RACQUETBALL CLUB
390 N.W.2d 212
Court of Appeals of Michigan
April 21, 1986

FACTS. The plaintiff was injured in a game of walleyball at Keatington Racquetball Club. Walleyball is volleyball played on a racquetball court. The rules of walleyball specify that it should be played with each team consisting of two, three, or four players.

The plaintiff filed a negligence action alleging the racquetball club had allowed five people to play on a team, thus overcrowding the court. The court dismissed the claim, ruling that the club did not owe a duty of supervision.

ISSUE. The court stated:

"The sole question before us is whether a recreational facility and its agents owe a duty to its members or customers to supervise informal games to ensure compliance with the games' rules. . ." (p. 213)

DECISION. A recreational facility has a duty to supervise informal games only when:

1. there is a contract providing the proprietor will supervise such activity,

2. the participants are children, or

3. the dangerous nature of the activity has the inherent potential to cause harm to the participant.

In the absence of those conditions, a recreational facility only owes a duty to maintain the premises free of defects. There is no obligation to supervise the informal games of patrons.

The concept of duty is when a person is under an obligation for the benefit of another; duty requires reasonable *conduct* which is what a person must or must not do, regarding another person.

Although a facility operator must take reasonable precaution for user safety, the issue is, again, one of foreseeability. Is the activity one which the facility expects will occur on its premises? If so, have there been previous injuries as a result of the activity? The facility operator's awareness of the potential risks and appreciation of the past problems created by those risks, determines the duty of supervision as in *Curtis v. State of Ohio.*

Wire-reinforced glass doors in a university field house does not create unreasonable danger unless the university failed to comply with building codes, or has notice of potential dangers.

CURTIS V. STATE OF OHIO
504 N.E.2d 1222
Court of Appeals of Ohio, Franklin Co.
September 18, 1986

FACTS. A member of the Ohio State University football team was running wind sprints with the team inside French Field House. During a sprint, he ran past the running area and broke through a wire-reinforced glass door with his leg.

The athlete filed suit against the university for its negligence in maintaining an unreasonably dangerous door and for maintaining a nuisance (a safety glass door could have reduced, if not eliminated, the extent of his injuries). The court rejected his claim and granted judgment to the university.

ISSUE. Should the university have installed safety glass doors?

DECISION. The court noted:

"Student-athletes training in university athletic facilities are owed the ordinary standard of care due invitees." (p. 1223)

Therefore, the university owed the athlete a duty to exercise ordinary or reasonable care in maintaining safe premises, to inspect for dangerous conditions, and to take reasonable precaution to protect him from foreseeable dangers. However, the athlete failed to prove that the university knew the door was a dangerous condition, that the wire-reinforced glass failed to comply with pertinent building codes and regulations, or that there were other similar injuries for which the university would have notice of an unreasonable risk of harm.

A nuisance can be intentional or negligent. The actions of the university were not *intentional*, that is, its actions were not reckless or unlawful.

PROTECTING CHILDREN

Providing for the safety of children is a difficult task because of the added supervision. However, the law has simplified its approach to the duty of care owed to children. Doctrines such as "attractive nuisance" are giving way to more traditional and usual applications of general negligence law. The ability of children, due to their age and maturity, to perceive and avoid risks or dangers is given more credence by the courts in weighing liability.

The primary consideration for establishing a facility's liability for a child's injury is foreseeability. The foreseeability factor imposes liability on a facility which was aware, or should have been aware, of unreasonably dangerous hazards that were likely sources of harm to children. Regarding children, the forseeability factor assumes that operators realize that children may not recognize unreasonable dangers or hazards. Even if the children did recognize the danger, they may not have the maturity to extricate themselves from the situation. In *Alop by Alop v. Edgewood Valley Community Association* and *Durham v. Forest Preserve District of Cook County*, the unreasonable dangers were created by the children, not the facility.

A playground slide situated on an asphalt surface is not a dangerous condition for children.

ALOP BY ALOP V. EDGEWOOD VALLEY COMMUNITY
ASSOCIATION
507 N.E.2d 19
Appellate Court of Illinois, 1st District
March 16, 1987

FACTS. A six-year-old girl was severely injured when she fell from a slide placed on an asphalt surface. The child, playing with a friend and without adult supervision, attempted to turn around in the middle of the slide and fell to the asphalt, suffering a fractured skull.

Her parent's lawsuit against the slide manufacturer and the owners of the premises was dismissed when the court ruled that the slide did not constitute a dangerous condition and that the defendants did not owe a duty of care to the child who was permitted to play without adult supervision.

ISSUE. What duties of care do the land owners owe to the child?

DECISION. In Illinois, children's rights to protection are the same as adults. There is not a duty requiring any greater precaution for their safety, except for dangerous conditions.

The key to determining liability for a child's injury is foreseeability. If a land owner maintains a dangerous condition in an area frequented by children and a child is injured as a result of the dangerous condition, then the land owner is liable.

In this case, it was known that children frequented the area; the only issue was whether the asphalt constituted a dangerous condition. The court ruled it did not since the child testified she knew it was dangerous to turn on the slide and that she knew she would be hurt if she fell onto the asphalt. The court also measured the apparent danger to the child by noting that she was allowed to play unsupervised.

> "It is always unfortunate when a child gets injured while playing, but a person who is merely in possession and control of the property cannot be required to indemnify against every possibility of injury thereon. The responsbility for a child's safety lies primarily with its parents, whose duty it is to see that his behavior does not involve danger to himself." (p. 23)

There is no duty to protect children from open and obvious dangers of which they are aware and can appreciate.

DURHAM V. FOREST PRESERVE DISTRICT OF COOK COUNTY
504 N.E.2d 899
Appellate Court of Illinois, 1st District
February 10, 1987

FACTS. A 16-year-old boy skipped school with a classmate and went to Schiller Woods Forest Preserve (Illinois). After drinking some beer, the boys carried a picnic table to Schiller Pond, and threw it in the water to raft. There were "No Swimming" signs posted. During horse-play on the "raft," the teenager fell into the water and drowned.

The boy's mother filed a claim charging the Forest Preserve with wilful and wanton misconduct in the operation of the Pond. However, the court ruled there was no duty of care owed to her son since the pond presented an open and obvious danger of which he should have been aware. The court dismissed the case.

ISSUE. An occupier or owner of land is required to remedy conditions which, though harmless to adults, are dangerous to children who may foreseeably wander onto the premises. Was this unfortunate result foreseeable?

DECISION. If an owner knows or should know that children frequent the premises *and* if the cause of the child's injury was the dangerous condition, the owner will be liable under the terms of ordinary negligence. However, a dangerous condition does not impose a duty on owners to repair the conditions when the risks of danger can be appreciated and avoided by children.

Because the boy was high school age, he was old enough to be allowed at large, and could appreciate the risks presented by Schiller Pond:

> "Moreover, 'any child of age to be allowed at large,' is expected to appreciate an obvious and open danger." (p. 902)

The Court examined an Illinois statute that provided a public entity owed a duty of ordinary care to persons whom the entity intended and permitted to use its property. Since the pond was clearly used for fishing, not swimming and because picnic tables were not intended to be used as rafts, the teenager was not within the class of people intended to use the property. Therefore, no duty of care was owed.

WILFUL AND WANTON MISCONDUCT

A consistently misunderstood area of tort liability is wilful and wanton misconduct. The name alone conveys a conduct beyond mere legal negligence. However, debate centers on its relationship to intentional tort acts, not negligence. (The word "intentional" in this context is actually misleading, because a wrongdoer's conduct does not have to be intentional to constitute wilful and wanton misconduct. Reckless conduct, also distinguished from intentional conduct, is conduct that has a likely probability of resulting harm to a user). The legal definition of wilful and wanton misconduct falls between intentional acts of harm and reckless conduct. For example, a facility operator who is aware of a dangerous condition or situation that threatens the facility users, is liable for wanton and wilful misconduct if he or she does not repair the condition or warn the users of its risks. The operator's failure to act, though not intended to harm the users, was an intentional disregard for their safety.

It should be assumed that any reputable recreational facility would not take part in any practices that would consititute an intentional harm to a patron. However, there are circumstances where a facility may be considered to have acted in reckless disregard of a user's safety. Therefore, it is important to understand the elements of wilful and wanton misconduct and to realize the legal consequences of that misconduct.

The facility operator must be cognizant of warning signs that threaten a user's safety. The operator has the duty to be aware of dangers or defects on the premises; that duty extends to dangers or defects that reasonably should have been discovered. The foreseeability factor becomes a very important consideration. When a facility operator discovers hazards to the facility users and fails to affirmatively or actively warn, repair, or react to the danger, the issue is no longer one of negligence, but of wilful and wanton misconduct.

A facility's failure to affirmatively react to dangers can occur in many subtle ways. For instance, were there previous injuries or accidents resulting from the risk or danger? Did the operator have knowledge of similar accidents or injuries at other facilities? If so, did the facility assume the affirmative duty to warn of the danger? Did the facility repair the hazard or defect? The failure to react to known and obvious hazards and dangers may not be intended to harm a facility user; however, it is an intentional disregard for the user's safety.

The facility operator is negligent when he or she fails to exercise ordinary care. Wilful and wanton misconduct is a more severe form of the lack of ordinary care that amounts to an intentional disregard, or utter indifference, for the user's safety. In *Miller v. Gibson*, a student alleged that a school's failure to provide bleacher side rails was wilful and wanton misconduct, not just negligence.

A school board's failure to install side rails on gym bleachers for a student assembly is not wilful and wanton misconduct.

MILLER V. GIBSON
355 S.E.2d 28
Supreme Court of Appeals of West Virginia
March 11, 1987

FACTS. During a student assembly at Point Pleasant High School (West Virginia), a student fell (or was pushed) from the bleachers in the school gymnasium. The student grabbed a teacher as he fell, and pulled her to the gym floor. The teacher sued the student; the student then sued the school board for reimbursment of any damages for which he might be liable to the teacher. The student alleged that the board was liable for wilful, wanton, and reckless misconduct in failing to install the detachable side guard rails to the bleachers.

The jury awarded the teacher $100,000 from the student, and awarded the student $99,000 from the school board. However, the West Virginia Supreme Court of Appeals overturned the jury verdict against the school, ruling that its actions might be negligent, but were not wilful, wanton, and reckless misconduct.

ISSUE. Exclusive of workmen's compensation benefits, West Virginia law provides that an injured employee may sue his or her employer only when the employee's injury was caused by the employer's wilful, wanton, and reckless misconduct. Was the school board's failure to install the side rails wilful, wanton, and reckless misconduct?

DECISION. The school board may have been negligent in failing to attach the guard rails, but there were no previous or similar injuries from which the board could have knowledge of any high degree of risk of physical harm to the teacher. Without that knowledge, the board could not be held liable for wilful, wanton, and reckless misconduct.

The school is not liable for injuries suffered by the teacher. It is not liable for reimbursement to the student because the board's actions were not wilful, wanton, and reckless misconduct.

The court noted:

> ". . . in an action in which his employee is the plaintiff, an employer may be liable in contribution to a third party as a joint tortfeasor only if the employer is guilty of wilful, wanton, and reckless misconduct proximately causing his employee's injury or death." (p. 32)

The liability aspect of wilful and wanton misconduct by a facility can be devastating. In Chapter Two, "Immunity Applications," we will see that immunity is not a valid legal defense to wilful and wanton misconduct. A facility cannot relieve itself of liability for its wilful and wanton misconduct by waivers of liability agreements. Wilful and wanton misconduct resulted in the theater being held liable for punitive damages, as well as compensatory damages, in *Jacobs v. Commonwealth Highland Theatres, Inc.* (Compensatory damages are awarded as a money substitute for the costs of a personal injury or property loss caused by another's negligence. Punitive damages are additional moneys which may be awarded to punish or deter intentional misconduct.)

The repeated failure to correct a dangerous theater step is a basis for awarding punitive damages.

JACOBS V. COMMONWEALTH HIGHLAND THEATRES, INC.
738 P.2d 6
Colorado Court of Appeals, Div. III
October 30, 1986

FACTS. The plaintiff, walking down the center aisle of the defendant's theater, stumbled on a step and fell. She fractured her leg and suffered permanent damage. She sued the defendant, and received a jury award of $100,000 for compensatory damages, and $150,000 for punitive damages.

The defendant appealed that the trial court erred in admitting evidence of prior, similar accidents and that the plaintiff failed to establish a case for the award of punitive damages. The court rejected the appeal.

ISSUE. When is evidence of similar injuries admissible? Does evidence of similar injuries establish negligence on the part of the defendant?

DECISION. The evidence disclosed that the theater was dark, the step was not well lit, the warning signs were inadequate, the ushers usually forgot to warn patrons of the step, and the carpet was so dark that it gave an impression of a ramp rather than a step. In the four years prior to the accident, there had been 10 falls on the step, some resulting in injury to patrons. The defendant was aware of the danger, and took no corrective measures to fix the step, other than to install some additional lighting.

The evidence of similar falls *alone* cannot establish negligence on the part of the defendant. However, the court admitted the evidence because it showed the continued existence of a dangerous condition of which defendant had notice, and created an attendant duty of care and safety for the patrons.

Punitive damages may be awarded only in instances of wanton and wilful disregard of the injured party, not for negligence. The defendant's repeated failure to take corrective measures and its purposeful failure to act, converted negligent conduct to wanton and wilful disregard.

ASSUMING THE RISK OF INJURY

Sport and recreational facilities have a specific interest in the legal defense of assumption of risk. Many sports have long been considered inherently dangerous activities. Traditionally, facility operators have been held to owe no duty or a minimal duty of care to participants and spectators at inherently dangerous sports. A participant or spectator who assumes the risk of injury from an inherently dangerous sport cannot recover damages for any injury suffered during the activity.

The two "no recovery" defenses, assumption of risk and contributory negligence, have been severely limited by the Doctrine of Comparative Negligence. Assumption of risk means the facility operator owes no duty of care, or a minimal duty of care at best to the user. Traditionally, if a facility operator owed a duty of care, the operator was not liable under contributory negligence if it was proved that the user's own negligence contributed or caused his or her injury. However, a majority of states now have comparative negligence statutes.

Under comparative negligence, the jury may allocate a percentage of fault to the plaintiff or the defendant, then award a damage accordingly. For example, if a jury found that a user had been injured suffering damages in the amount of $10,000 and that the facility's negligence was 60 percent of the cause, and the user's negligence was 40 percent of the cause of the injury, the user would be awarded $6,000.

Assumption of risk does not apply to a death resulting from a shallow-water dive.

MURRAY V. RAMADA INN, INC.
821 F.2d 272
United States Court of Appeals, 5th Cir.
July 13, 1987

FACTS. The decedent was performing shallow water dives in a swimming pool managed by the defendant. He struck his head on the bottom of the pool, and was paralyzed. He later died as a result of the injury. His widow and child filed a lawsuit, alleging the defendant operated the pool in an unreasonably dangerous manner since a lifeguard was not present and for failing to warn of the dangers of shallow water dives. The defendant countered that the decedent had assumed the risk of injury by shallow water diving.

The jury returned a verdict finding the decedent and the defendant were equally negligent (comparative negligence), and awarded the decedent's heirs a total of $250,000, or 50 percent of the damages resulting from his death.

ISSUE. The defendant appealed the verdict, arguing the jury should have been instructed to consider assumption of risk (a complete bar to any money recovery), and it should not have been permitted to consider comparative negligence (allocation of damages based on percentage of fault).

DECISION. Under Louisiana law, assumption of risk is subject to comparative negligence. The dispute was whether one who assumes a risk of injury is completely barred from recovery under the negligence theory. Because the evidence regarding negligence was conflicting, the jury had the right to determine that the defendant's negligence contributed to the decedent's death.

In Louisiana, the assumption of risk defense is *subsumed* (emphasis added) by the defense of comparative negligence.

The no recovery feature of contributory negligence has been changed to a reduction of recovery concept. Assumption of risk may be effectively eliminated by the adoption of comparative negligence.

Implied Assumption of Risk

Many assumption of risk relationships and situations are not delineated by written agreements, called waivers of liability. In the absence of an agreement, implied assumption of risk has been applied where the injured party was aware of the risk of injury, understood and appreciated the risk, and voluntarily chose to encounter the risk.

A college athlete who ran into the dark, unlit grounds of a motel during a water fight assumed the risk of injury.

VENTURA V. WINEGARDNER
357 S.E.2d 764
Supreme Court of Appeals of West Virginia
May 15, 1987

FACTS. The plaintiff, a college senior and member of the Rutgers University tennis team, was at West Virginia University for a tennis tournament. Her team was staying at the defendant's Holiday Inn in Star City, West Virginia.

The teammates started a water fight. During the horseplay, the plaintiff, while attempting to run away from some friends, ran into an unlit area beyond the motel walkway, and fell down a steep embankment. She suffered a knee injury that ended her competitive tennis career. The West Virginia Supreme Court reversed the jury's award to the athlete because the trial court had not allowed the jury to consider whether the plaintiff assumed the risk of injury.

ISSUE. If the plaintiff assumed the risk of injury, she would be barred from recovering damages. What are the elements of assumption of risk? Why should the jury have been required to consider assumption of risk?

DECISION. The court cited the elements of assumption of risk as:

"(1) knowledge of the danger; (2) an appreciation of the danger, and (3) voluntary exposure to the danger." (p. 767)

The court cited cases where running with bare feet on wet pavement and walking into an unlit areas were acts of assumption of risk.

The plaintiff was aware of the surroundings since she passed the embankment in daylight hours. She ran into an unlit area at a full sprint which was a danger a reasonable person could appreciate, and to which she voluntarily exposed herself.

Any legal defense operating to completely bar any recovery for injury is controversial. In the case of implied assumption of risk, the controversy takes many forms. Should assumption of risk apply only when the recreational facility does not have a duty of care to the user? Does it apply when the facility has breached a duty of care? What duties of care, if any, are required for inherently dangerous sports or activities?

Assumption of Risk or Contributory Negligence? One of the most pressing judicial inquiries is the relationship of assumption of risk to contributory negligence in comparative negligence jurisdictions.

Contributory negligence is a proper defense in a comparative negligence jurisdiction.

RICHARDSON V. CLAYTON & LAMBERT
MANUFACTURING COMPANY
657 F.Supp. 751
U.S. District Court, N.D. Mississippi
January 20, 1987

FACTS. A swimmer, diving from the side of a pool toward the sloping deep end, was injured when he struck the bottom. He filed a negligence action against the pool manufacturer. The swimmer was familiar with the type of pool, knew that it was unsafe to dive in shallow water, but was unaware of anyone being injured by similar dives. He believed he was diving safely.

The manufacturer alleged the swimmer had assumed the risk of injury. The court disagreed and said the issue was one of contributory negligence and that the negligence of both the plaintiff and the defendant had to be considered.

ISSUE. What is the difference between the defense of assumption of risk, and the defense of contributory negligence?

DECISION. Assumption of risk is a complete bar to recovery; if the plaintiff is judged to have assumed a known risk, he cannot recover damages from the defendant. However, contributory negligence is no longer a complete bar to recovery. A majority of states have comparative negligence laws where the jury's duty is to compare the contributory negligence of the plaintiff, if any, against the negligence of the defendant in order to determine whether there will be a damage recovery.

The court determined that when the application of assumption of risk or contributory negligence is in issue, the jury should only be instructed about contributory negligence. The jury should not be instructed on assumption of risk since that defense would not allow them to compare "the respective negligence, if any, of the parties."

Statutory Assumption of Risk. Skiing has long been recognized as an inherently dangerous sport. In many states that garner ski industry revenues, laws have been passed that impose assumption of risk on skiers who are injured. The laws in Michigan and Montana were upheld in *Grieb v. Alpine Valley Ski Area, Inc.* and *Kelleher v. Big Sky of Montana.*

A Michigan statute that recognizes collision as an inherent danger of skiing has a legitimate objective and purpose.

GRIEB V. ALPINE VALLEY SKI AREA, INC.
400 N.W.2d 653
Court of Appeals of Michigan
October 20, 1986

FACTS. The plaintiff collided with another skier while skiing at Alpine Valley Ski Resort (Michigan). She filed a lawsuit against Alpine Valley which the court dismissed based on a Michigan statute which stated, in part:

> "Each person who participates in the sport of skiing accepts the dangers that inhere in that sport insofar as the dangers are obvious and necessary. Those dangers include . . . collisions . . . with other skiers." (p. 654)

The plaintiff believed that the law violated her constitutional rights of due process and equal protection of the laws.

ISSUE. The state law must have a legitimate state objective and must be rationally related to that legitimate objective.

DECISION. The statute is clear and unambiguous in its language regarding collision with another skier. A skier assumes collision with another skier as an obvious and necessary danger of the sport.

The assumption of the obvious and necessary dangers is a rational solution for the need to promote safety, and to limit the amount of potential liability facing operators. The plaintiff failed to carry her burden of proving that the statute had no public purpose or that no reasonable relationship existed between the statute and the purpose to be served.

The court added:

> "Plaintiff's argument that the safety of the citizen is a higher interest than the economic well-being of the ski industry and the state, so that the latter interests must give way to the former, goes to the wisdom of the legislation, not the constitutionality." (p. 656)

A state law that imposes assumption of risk on skiers does not prevent an injured skier from filing a proper negligence claim.

KELLEHER V. BIG SKY OF MONTANA
642 F.Supp. 1128
United States District Court, D. Montana
September 5, 1986

Montana law provides, in part:

> "A skier assumes the risk and all legal responsibility for injury to himself or loss of property that results from participating in the sport of skiing by virtue of his participation. The assumption of risk and responsibility includes but is not limited to injury or loss caused by the following: variations in terrain, surface or subsurface snow or ice conditions, bare spots, rocks, trees, other forms of forest growth or debris, lift towers and components thereof, pole lines, and plainly marked or visible snowmaking equipment." (p. 1129)

FACTS. The plaintiff was injured in an avalanche while sking on the premises of Big Sky of Montana. He filed a lawsuit for damages, but Big Sky contended that the plaintiff assumed the risks of injury inherent to skiing, including avalanche.

The plaintiff asked the trial court to declare the statute unconstitutional because it would operate as a bar to his recovery; thus, it would violate his fundamental right of access to the courts. The court denied the plaintiff's motion.

ISSUE. What effect does the Montana Statute have regarding either the plaintiff's right to sue, or the potential liability of Big Sky?

DECISION. The statute does not adversely affect plaintiff's right of access to the courts because it does not preclude him from bringing the suit itself, nor does it keep plaintiff from establishing negligence on the part of the defendant. The statute defines the risks of skiing, but negligence is not one of them. The filing of the action and the ability to recover damages, are not limited if his claim is presented "in a proper negligence case."

Minimal Duty of Care. The issue confronting many courts regarding inherently dangerous sports is whether the nature of the activity is such that facilities have no duties of care or, that there is a minimal duty of care. More than likely, the difference is one of semantics rather than substance. Those who advocate that there is no duty of care for inherently dangerous activities would probably accept two limitations: first, inherently dangerous sports require a minimal duty, but not the affirmative duty which is owed to invitees; and, the minimal duty should consist primarily of a danger or hazard warning. The courts pondered the issue of minimal duties owed to jockeys in *Thompson v. Ruidoso-Sunland, Inc.* and *Turcotte v. Fell*; to roller skaters in *Wagner v. Thomas J. Obert*; to baseball fans in *Friedman v. Houston Sports Association*; and, to golfers in *Potter v. Green Meadows, Par 3.*

An unsafe inside rail at a race track is not a known danger for which jockeys assume the risk of injury.

THOMPSON V. RUIDOSO-SUNLAND, INC.
734 P.2d 267
Court of Appeals of New Mexico
February 17, 1987

FACTS. A jockey's horse was bumped during a race causing the jockey to fall against the metal pole used to anchor the inside rail of the track. The inside rail, called a "gooseneck" rail, was a known safety hazard, and was to be replaced with a safer rail at the close of the racing season.

The jockey sued the the owner of the race track to recover for the severe injuries he suffered. However, the court determined that the owner, and the jockey were each 50 percent negligent, and that the owner was not guilty of wanton and wilful misconduct for failing to replace the rail.

ISSUE. Did the owner of the track owe a duty of care to the jockey? Did the jockey assume the risk of collision with the rail?

DECISION. Primary assumption of risk means that the owner would have no duty of care to the jockey at all; secondary assumption of risk implies there is a duty of care which has been breached, but for which assumption of risk can be a defense.

The court determined that the track owner did owe a duty of care to the jockey because the dangerous rail was not a known and inherent danger to horse racing.

Though the owner was aware of the danger presented by the gooseneck rail, it was acknowledged that he intended to replace it at the end of the season. Therefore, his actions were not considered to be reckless, or willful and wanton misconduct.

Secondary assumption of risk of injury was a valid defense by the owner. Thus, the court could properly compare the negligence of the owner to the negligence, if any, of the jockey. In this case, the evidence supported the 50-50 finding.

Horse racing is an inherently dangerous sport; therefore, jockeys assume the risk of injury caused by an opponent's careless riding.

TURCOTTE V. FELL
502 N.E.2d 964
Court of Appeals of New York
November 25, 1986

FACTS. The plaintiff was a famed jockey for 17 years. His career was ended when his horse clipped the heels of another horse in a race at Belmont Park. He was thrown from the horse, and rendered quadriplegic as a result of the fall. He claimed that the jockey on the other horse caused the accident by "foul riding" in violation of racing rules.

The plaintiff filed an action against the jockey and the owner of the other horse and against the track operator for negligent maintenance of the track. The court dismissed the case because the only duty of the track was to refrain from reckless or intentionally harmful conduct.

ISSUE. Assumption of risk includes incidental risks that are fully comprehended or obvious to the participant. Is a foul committed by another participant in horse racing an accepted, incidental risk of horse racing?

DECISION. A participant in an inherently dangerous sport does not consent to reckless or intentional acts. However, though rules prohibiting foul riding are safety rules, those infractions do not constitute intentional or reckless conduct when committed as a result of carelessness. The foul riding here was distinguished from a "flagrant foul," which is unrelated to the race or game and done without competitive purpose.

Horse racing is an inherently dangerous sport that involves bumping and jostling of the mounts; the failure to control a horse is carelessness, not reckless or intentional conduct.

The track operator is not negligent since the conditions of the track were common to the conditions found on most tracks and because the plaintiff had ridden three races at the same track that day prior to the injury. He was well aware of the dangers, and had accepted the risk.

Primary assumption of risk is distinguished from secondary assumption of risk for a skater's injury at a roller skating rink.

WAGNER V. THOMAS J. OBERT
396 N.W.2d 223
Supreme Court of Minnesota
November 21, 1986

FACTS. A skater was injured at the defendant's roller skating rink. She alleged that she fell while trying to reach the lobby from the skating floor that was crowded with unsupervised children. She also contended the fall may have resulted from a bent, concave metal ramp connecting the rink floor and the lobby. The owner of the skating rink produced conflicting accounts of the accident.

When she lost her lawsuit, the plaintiff claimed the court had confused the jury regarding assumption of risk. The court rejected her claim.

ISSUE. What standards of care were owed by the operator to the plaintiff? When does a patron of the roller skating rink assume risk of injury?

DECISION. The management owes its patrons a duty to safely supervise and maintain its premises. However, a patron using the premises may be said to have assumed the risk of injury resulting from *well-known, incidental* (emphasis added) risks; the management cannot be deemed negligent since it does not owe a duty of care for those risks in the first place. This is called primary assumption of risk and is usually applied in cases involving inherently dangerous sporting events.

Secondary risk occurs when the patron is placed in danger by the negligence of the defendant, yet voluntarily chooses to encounter the known and appreciated danger regardless of the risk.

Ordinarily, the negligent maintenance and supervision of a skating rink are not inherent dangers to the sport of roller skating.

A stadium has a limited duty to provide screened seats for patrons attending a baseball game.

FRIEDMAN V. HOUSTON SPORTS ASSOCIATION
731 S.W.2d 572
Court of Appeals of Texas, Houston
March 5, 1987

FACTS. An 11-year-old girl, attending a baseball game at the Houston Astrodome with her father, was struck near the right eye by a foul ball. They sat in seats unprotected by screens behind the first base dugout. During the last inning of the game, the youngster walked down directly behind the dugout where she was hit by the ball. The defendant, owner of the Astrodome, was sued by the youngster's father.

The court granted judgment to the defendant notwithstanding the fact that a jury was prepared to award the girl and her father damages in the amount of $170,000 on their negligence claim.

ISSUE. Is there a duty to warn baseball fans of the dangers of foul balls? What duties of protection does a stadium operator owe to baseball patrons?

DECISION. A stadium operator has the duty to exercise reasonable care to protect patrons from injury. In the case of foul balls, most jurisdictions have adopted the rule that a stadium operator only owes a *limited* (emphasis added) duty to provide enough screened seats for fans who desire them. There is not a duty to patrons who choose to sit in unscreened areas. The law in Texas, as well as most states, does not require the operator to warn fans of the dangers of foul balls.

A concurring judge was concerned whether there should be a duty to warn children who may not be aware of the dangers of baseball. However, the judge agreed there was no duty to warn because the child had been accompanied by an adult responsible for her welfare.

A golfer does not assume risk of injury from a ricocheted golf ball unless he has actual knowledge of a danger at the tee area.

POTTER V. GREEN MEADOWS, PAR 3
510 So.2d 1225
District Court of Appeal of Florida
August 13, 1987

FACTS. The plaintiff was playing golf at the defendant's par three course. The tee areas were originally installed with 5 ft. x 5 ft. concrete slabs covered with a rubber strip holding a tee. Over the years, the tees were worn away or knocked away, and the tee slabs became unusable. As was the practice of many golfers, the plaintiff teed off behind the tee slab on the fourth hole. The concrete slab was not visible because it was set further in the ground than other slabs, and was covered with weeds.

The plaintiff's tee shot struck the slab, ricocheted back, and hit him in the eye, causing severe injury.

The trial court believed the plaintiff had assumed the risk of injury. However, the Florida District Court of Appeal disagreed and sent the case back for a new trial since there was a question if the course had been negligently maintained.

ISSUE. Does the golf course have a duty to protect golfers from being struck by a ricocheting golf ball?

DECISION. There is a duty by a landowner who provides a sport facility to exercise reasonable care to prevent foreseeable injuries to participants and to anticipate that participants may risk a known danger anyway. In this case, the evidence showed that the slab was camouflaged by weeds; the plaintiff may not have had actual knowledge of its danger.

NOTE: In Florida, *express assumption of risk* requires that the defendant prove the plaintiff had actual knowledge of the risk giving rise to the injury.

Express Assumption of Risk

The validity of waivers of liability (exculpatory agreemeents) is often questioned. Exculpatory agreements, however, generally remain enforceable instruments. It is the recognized right of a user to execute a contract which relieves a facility from potential liability due to its negligent conduct.

However, the courts scrutinize such agreements to insure they are clearly understood by the forgiving party[2], that the agreement refers to the area of risks for which the forgiving party is releasing a claim, and that the agreement does not violate a public policy. In *Williams v.*

United States, the court examined whether public policy allowed the government to escape liability for the death of a teenage swimmer. In *Lohman v. Peoria Speedway, Inc.*, the court examined the legal conditions for a valid waiver.

Waiver of liability releasing the government for its negligent care of a 16-year-old R.O.T.C. student violates public policy.

WILLIAMS V. UNITED STATES
660 F.Supp. 699
U. S. District Court, E.D. Arkansas
May 7, 1987

FACTS. A 16-year-old high school R.O.T.C. student attended a summer leadership school sponsored by the United States Air Force. During a swimming party, he did a swan dive from a high diving board. The three lifeguards on duty did not see him enter the water and at least four minutes elapsed from the time he would have entered the water until his body was pulled from the bottom of the pool. An additional 30 seconds elapsed before effective cardio-pulmonary resuscitation was administered. Although he was briefly resuscitated, the student ultimately died of brain damage due to the lack of oxygen.

His family was granted a judgment against the government which contended it was exempt from liability by a waiver of liability (exculpatory agreement) signed by the father.

ISSUE. Waivers of liability must be clear and definite and must not violate public policy; they are strictly construed against the party seeking release from liability.

DECISION. The court determined that the waiver was invalid since it was unclear the government intended to relieve itself from its own wrongful conduct. The court found inconsistencies when the Air Force form contained language such as "supervised" activities, and "in the unlikely event of injury," which appeared to promise responsible care. In fact, the student's death was caused by the lack of observation for an unreasonable time by the lifeguards.

The court determined that the lack of attention by the lifeguards to the student when he entered the water, the failure of the lifeguards to monitor the diving area according to the pool rules, and the lack of training which delayed effective CPR, directly caused the teenager's death.

Additionally, public policy was violated because:

> "To permit the Government to assume the care and custody of school children without an underlying policy encouraging the exercise of reasonable care would violate basic principles of fairness." (p. 703)

A waiver of liability is valid against the claim of an injured pit crew member.

LOHMAN V. PEORIA SPEEDWAY, INC.
497 N.E.2d 143
Appellate Court of Illinois
August 21, 1986

FACTS. While removing debris from the auto race track at Peoria Speedway, the plaintiff, a member of a pit crew, was struck by a race car. Prior to the race, the plaintiff and the race car driver each executed a waiver:

> " . . . releasing Peoria Speedway from . . . any and all claims and liabilities . . . arising out of their activities at the Peoria Speedway."

The plaintiff sued the speedway and the race car driver for damages. The driver then sued the speedway asking to be indemnified for any amounts he may be liable to the plaintiff. The court dismissed both suits against the speedway ruling that it was protected from liability by valid releases.

ISSUE. What is the effect of the waiver of liability?

DECISION. If the release agreement does not violate public policy and is executed in the absence of a special relationship requiring enforcement (e.g., common carrier or employer-employee), parties are free to contract their own affairs, including relief from their own negligence.

These agreements have been upheld to protect track owners from the claims of drivers and participants. The track was neither liable to the plaintiff based on the signed release, nor liable to the driver for indemnification.

STADIUM AND ARENA ISSUES

This last section presents five cases dealing with stadium and arena issues.

Construction and Design Liabilities

Cincinnati Riverfront Coliseum, Inc. v. McNulty Co. examined the liability of architects or structural engineers for faulty construction design. Expert opinions regarding the cause of stadium construction defects are legally privileged communications according to the court in *Western Technologies, Inc. v. Sverdrup & Parcel, Inc.*

An architect or structural engineer is responsible to exercise reasonable care in the preparation of facility designs.

CINCINNATI RIVERFRONT COLISEUM, INC. V. McNULTY CO.
504 N.E.2d 415
Supreme Court of Ohio
December 26, 1986

FACTS. The Cincinnati Riverfront Coliseum, Inc. contracted with the defendant, a structural engineering firm, to build an outdoor walkway for coliseum pedestrian traffic. The defendant performed all structural engineering services, including the design of the walkway. The actual construction was performed by three independent contractors. The city of Cincinnati agreed to provide all the necessary maintenance and repair services. Within five years after construction, the walkway had suffered extensive water damage and deterioration.

The coliseum filed an action against the 11 parties involved in the construction of the walkway, including the defendant.

ISSUE. What duties of care does the defendant, as structural engineer for the project, owe to the coliseum?

DECISION. An architect or structural engineer is liable for the foreseeable consequences of failing to exercise reasonable care in the preparation of the design. However, the architect will not be held liable for negligence if there are "material" construction deviations from the design which cause the damage.

A deviation in construction is considered "material" when it completely removes the effects of any negligence on the part of the architect or structural engineer in the preparation of the design.

The defendant admitted that its design did not take into account the exposure to weather, or the walkway's ability to disperse surface water. The court rejected the defendant's argument that there were material deviations from its design in the actual construction of the walkway.

Expert opinions regarding stadium construction defects are legally privileged communications.

WESTERN TECHNOLOGIES, INC. V. SVERDRUP & PARCEL, INC.
739 P.2d 1318
Court of Appeals of Arizona
October 16, 1986

FACTS. The plaintiff was retained by Arizona State University to perform engineering services in the expansion of Sun Devil Stadium. After completion of the expansion in the late 1970s, cracks developed in the stadium. Arizona State then hired the defendant to determine the cause of the problems. The defendant reported that the plaintiff's work, in part, caused the damage. Arizona State filed a lawsuit against the plaintiff for damages which was settled by the parties.

Later, the plaintiff filed this suit against the defendant alleging that the defendant had negligently, recklessly, or intentionally supplied Arizona State with false information regarding plaintiff's work. The court, however, ruled that the information provided to Arizona State by the defendant was privileged, and dismissed the claim.

ISSUE. The defense of absolute privilege protects conduct for which one would otherwise be liable since the conduct itself is in furtherance of some socially important interest protected by law. How does absolute privilege apply to this case?

DECISION. Absolute privilege protects participants in judicial proceedings to insure the complete exposure of pertinent information for the prosecution or defense of a lawsuit. That purpose is considered a socially important interest to be protected by law. Therefore, the court had to determine whether the defendant's status as a potential witness in the lawsuit filed by Arizona State against the plaintiff fell within the absolute privilege category. (Generally, privilege applies to all steps of a legal proceeding, but not to statements made before or after the legal proceeding.)

The defendant's statements to Arizona State were made prior to the filing of Arizona State's lawsuit; nevertheless, they were made while that suit was being seriously considered. Also, the lawsuit could not be filed until Arizona State had the defendant's assessment. Thus, the defendant's statements to Arizona State were "a necessary step in taking legal action." Since Arizona State relied on the defendant's statements in bringing the suit, the information was privileged communication.

Lease Agreements

The scope of a lease agreement for stadium advertising space was considered in *Keating v. Stadium Management Corporation.*

Rental agreement for stadium advertising space is ambiguous.

KEATING V. STADIUM MANAGEMENT CORPORATION
508 N.E.2d 121
Appeals Court of Massachusetts
June 2, 1987

FACTS. Plaintiff was the Director of Operations at Schaefer Stadium (since renamed Sullivan Stadium, home of the New England Patriots). The stadium was managed by Stadium Realty Trust. The plaintiff entered into an agreement with the Philip Morris Company to lease stadium space for Marlboro cigarette advertisements. Under the terms of the lease, the plaintiff would receive a 15 percent commission from rental payments received for the initial term of the lease, and 10 percent commission from rental payments for any extension or subsequent leases with Philip Morris. The agreement was signed and approved by the Trust.

Plaintiff received his commissions until 1981 when the defendant, who succeeded the Trust, stopped the rental commissions to the plaintiff, citing a paragraph in the lease agreement that stated, in part:

> "Keating shall not be entitled to commissions on account of rentals . . . from any business . . . which has in the past purchased advertising space or time from any lessee of the Trust."

The defendant argued that no further commissions were due because Philip Morris had purchased advertisement space in the New England Patriots football game program since 1971, prior to the date of the lease agreement with the Trust. The defendant then negotiated a new agreement with Philip Morris for advertising space.

Plaintiff sued the defendant for breach of contract and was granted judgment for 10 percent of all rental payments due under the subsequent agreement with Philip Morris.

ISSUE. Defendant contended that the language of the contract speaks for itself, and the court should not consider any evidence other than the precise language of the contract.

DECISION. There was no question that the Trust sought in-stadium advertising from Philip Morris without reference to game program advertisements; the lease terminology referred to signs in the stadium or on the message board. Further, for the five years prior to the defendant's termination of the commissions, there had never been any issue regarding the payment of commissions due the plaintiff.

The court ruled that the language of the section of the lease agreement in question was ambiguous. Accordingly, it considered evidence other than the precise language of the lease.

Insurance

In *Ross v. City of Minneapolis*, the liability insurance coverage for the Minneapolis Auditorium excluded injuries to spectators from assault and battery.

Liability insurance for the Minneapolis Auditorium excludes injuries resulting from assault and battery.

ROSS V. CITY OF MINNEAPOLIS
408 N.W.2d 910
Court of Appeals of Minnesota
July 7, 1987

FACTS. A spectator leaving a wrestling match at the Minneapolis Auditorium was assaulted by unidentified persons. He lost his right eye as a result of the attack. Alleging the failure to take proper safety precautions for wrestling fans, he filed a suit against the city of Minneapolis, owner of the auditorium, as well as the club that sponsored the match.

A settlement agreement was reached whereby the spectator was to be awarded $500,000 payable by the city's insurance carrier. The trial court consented to the settlement. However, when the spectator tried to recover, the insurance company refused to pay, alleging that it was not party to the settlement, and that the injuries to the spectator were excluded from the coverage of the policy. The court of appeals agreed and reversed the settlement order of the trial court.

ISSUE. The language of the policy stated that damages would be paid for injuries caused by an "occurrence," that is, an accident neither expected nor intended by the insured. However, the policy also contained an exclusion provision stating it would not pay for injuries "arising" out of an assault and battery. The spectator's suit alleged that his injuries were proximately caused by the *negligence* of the city and the club sponsor. Is the carrier liable for the injuries?

DECISION. The response of the court of appeals was short and concise. The language of the exclusion was plain and unambiguous. Injuries which arose from an assault and battery were excluded from coverage. It was error for the trial court to find coverage under the agreement based on negligence simply because that was the allegation of the injured party.

The insurance contract must be given its plain, ordinary, and popular meaning. The court cannot impose ambiguity into plain language of a contract "in order to construe it against the one who prepared the contract."

Independent Contractors

In *Vanchieri v. New Jersey Sports and Exposition Authority*, the independent contractor hired to provide safety and security at Giants Stadium did not share the same immunity protection granted to the Meadowlands.

An independent contractor hired by the Meadowlands to supervise safety and security is not protected by governmental immunity.

VANCHIERI V. NEW JERSEY SPORTS AND EXPOSITION
AUTHORITY
514 A.2d 1323
Supreme Court of New Jersey
September 30, 1986

FACTS. The plaintiff attended a pre-season football game at Giants Stadium, owned and operated by the Meadowlands. Following the game, the plaintiff was knocked down by a young man roughhousing near the exit. She suffered a hip injury which required insertion of a prosthetic replacement.

The plaintiff filed a lawsuit against the Meadowlands and against the independent contractor in charge of safety and security at the Meadowlands. The court ruled that the independent contractor was not protected by the same governmental immunity afforded the Meadowlands.

ISSUE. New Jersey law provided, in part, that a public entity (or its employees) was not liable for the failure to provide supervision at public recreational facilities. Is an independent contractor an employee for immunity purposes?

DECISION. The employees of the Meadowlands were protected by immunity. However, the statute was not so broadly interpreted that an independent contractor would be considered an employee for immunity purposes.

However, if the public entity provided the plans or specifications of operation for the contractor to follow and if the contractor followed the plans or specifications without deviation, then the independent contractor would not be held liable for any defective work. In this case, the Meadowlands had the right to supply plans or specifications, but there was no evidence to show that the Meadowlands exercised that power, or that the independent contractor complied with any such plans.

REFERENCES

Berry, R. and G. Wong. 1986. *Law and Business of the Sports Industries*. Vol. II: 279-303, 392-419. Dover, MA: Auburn House Publishing Co.

Kionka, E. 1977. *Torts: Injuries to Persons and Property*. Nutshell Series: 51-120, 210-243, 354-388. St. Paul, MN: West Publishing Co.

Practicing Comparative Fault. 1987. Indiana Continuing Legal Education Forum.

Prosser, W. 1984. *The Law of Torts*. W.P. Keeton 5th ed., 386-451. St. Paul, MN: West Publishing Co.

Schubert, G., R. Smith, and J. Trentadue. 1986. *Sports Law*. 232-272. St. Paul, MN: West Publishing Co.

Sweet, J. *Legal Aspects of Architecture, Engineering, and the Construction Process*. 3rd ed., 100-125. St. Paul, MN: West Publishing Co.

[1] The terms "property," "land," and "facility" are synonymous for this discussion. In addition, the terms "user" and "patron" are interchangeable, as well as "facility owner" and "facility operator."

The legal classifications for users is not affected by the choice of terms.

[2] Compare the decisions by the Illinois Appellate Court, in *Neuman v. Gloria Marshall Figure Salon*, 500 N.E.2d 1011 (Ill. App. Ct. 1986) and *Calarco v. YMCA of Greater Metropolitan Chicago*, 501 N.E.2d 268 (Ill. Ct. App. 1986). In *Neuman*, the court dismissed the lawsuit of a health club member who was injured on an exercise machine. The court said the injury had been reasonably contemplated according to the language of the waiver which stated, in part:.

"Patron specifically assumes all risk of injury while using any equipment or facilities at the salon . . ."

Five days later, in *Calarco* the Appellate Court ruled a waiver was invalid because the language of the agreement was *not* clear, specific, and unequivocal. The court found the language of the waiver to be confusing since it could apply equally to activities or equipment.

" . . . waive, release, and forever discharge any and all rights and claims for damages which I may have . . . arising out of or connected with my participation in any of the activities of the YMCA of Metropolitan Chicago."

Chapter 2

Immunity Applications

INTRODUCTION

Most legal topics discussed by attorneys are not chosen out of self-interest, but because those topics have the greatest impact on the specific industry. Immunity is one of those topics. This is readily evidenced by the number of cases reported in the last year applying governmental and/or recreational use immunity to recreational and sports-related industries.

Immunity is freedom from lawsuit or liability. We shall consider immunity as it relates to liability. Generally, immunity is justified by social values requiring governmental units to remain free of liability, regardless of their negligent wrongdoing. Those social values date back to the English common law which held that the king could not be sued. This immunity concept is called governmental or sovereign immunity, which are synonymous terms for our purposes.

As demonstrated in *Greenhill v. Carpenter* and *Smith v. Town of Dewey Beach*, governmental immunity has one primary purpose: protection of the public treasury.

A state university is immune from liability for the death of an athlete killed while representing the school on a recruiting trip.

GREENHILL V. CARPENTER
718 S.W.2d 268
Court of Appeals of Tennessee
July 1, 1986

FACTS. A football player at Memphis State University (MSU) was killed in a plane crash, with the football coach. They were on their way to a banquet. The player was accompanying the coach for recruiting purposes.

His mother filed suit against the university, the athletic department, the university president, athletic director, and the coach's estate for negligence and breach of contract. She alleged that she gave her consent for her son to attend MSU because the coach had represented that her son would be insured while he was a student-athlete at Memphis State.

The court dismissed the suit based on immunity granted to the university and its employees.

ISSUE. The Tennessee Immunity Statute states, in part:

> "Be it further enacted, that except where sovereign immunity has been or shall hereafter be expressly waived by the General Assembly, all appropriations of state revenues and departmental revenues . . . to the state, its departments, agencies, boards, educational institution, instrumentalities, and incorporated entities . . . shall be state funds and shall be protected by the state's sovereign immunity . . ." (p. 272)

DECISION. The operating funds of the athletic department were derived from sources other than tax revenues and were, ordinarily, private moneys. However, based on the immunity statute, the court considered the athletic funds as public funds, protected by immunity.

The Sovereign Immunity Statute specified that a lawsuit may be maintained against the state only with *express* approval of the legislature. And, officials of the state, acting in an official capacity, were entitled to immunity.

Memphis State University, as a state university, was liable only for *express* (written) contracts. Whether the coach's representation constituted an oral contract was immaterial because there was no *express* contract.

Delaware's Director of Parks and Recreation may personally claim the immunity protection granted to the state under the Eleventh Amendment.

SMITH V. TOWN OF DEWEY BEACH
659 F.Supp. 752
U. S. District Court, D. Delaware
May 1, 1987

FACTS. Two young men, while swimming in the ocean off Delaware beaches, dove and struck their heads on the ocean bottom resulting in severe and permanent injuries. Their families filed lawsuits against the Director of Parks and Recreation for the state of Delaware, and the towns of Dewey Beach and Bethany Beach.

The director argued that he was protected from the claims under immunity granted by the Eleventh Amendment. (This amendment grants immunity to states which are sued in federal courts.)

ISSUE. The state of Delaware was not named a defendant in the lawsuit. Since the suit named the director as a defendant, may he claim the same immunity protection granted to the state by the Eleventh Amendment?

DECISION. The state of Delaware, as a named defendant, could defend on the basis of Eleventh Amendment immunity. Eleventh Amendment immunity protection is granted when the state is the real, substantive party in interest to the suit. If any damages are payable from the state treasury, then the state is the real party in interest.

The Division of Parks and Recreation is authorized and funded through the Delaware Department of Natural Resources and Environmental Control (DNREC). The director helps prepare budget items for his division and DNREC funds come from the state. Any judgment against the director would have to be paid by the state. Therefore, the director is not precluded from Eleventh Amendment immunity protection.

The state of Delaware can waive immunity if it has an insurance program to protect it against a particular risk. However, such a waiver extends only to the state's sovereign immunity, it does not extend to Eleventh Amendment immunity rights.

Recreational use immunity is a derivative concept which is justified by social values relating to private landowners and their property. Its protection is limited to location and recreational use. Governmental immunity enjoys broader application; however, both concepts only apply to negligent conduct. A facility's wilful, wanton, or reckless misconduct is not protected by either immunity application.

In Chapter One, "Facility Management," we learned that negligent conduct was the failure to exercise reasonable or ordinary care. Wilful and wanton misconduct was a more severe conduct comprised of varying degrees of unreasonable risks, and a lack of appreciation for the dangers confronting users, amounting to an utter disregard for their safety.[1]

LIMITATIONS

There is a popular belief that immunity has been largely abolished in the United States in recent years. Obviously, the move to abolition was spurred by a basic concern for what is fair and equitable, especially when it related to the conduct of a public agency, or its employees. However, it is important to differentiate total abolition from mere limitation; what is perceived as legislative abolition is usually a limited application.

Insurance

Many states permit public agencies to purchase liability insurance policies. Generally, the purchase of liability insurance serves as a waiver of governmental immunity by the public agency. However, even in those circumstances, the courts are reluctant to recognize the purchase of such policies as a waiver of any immunity-protected status beyond the policy limits.[2] In *Antiporek v. Village of Hillside*, it was alleged that membership in a self-insurance group was a waiver of governmental immunity.

Municipal membership in a self-insurance group is not a waiver of governmental immunity.

ANTIPOREK V. VILLAGE OF HILLSIDE
499 N.E.2d 1308
Supreme Court of Illinois
May 21, 1986

FACTS. A young girl was injured while sledding on property owned and maintained by the Village of Hillside (Illinois). At the time of the accident, Hillside was a member of Intergovernmental Risk Management Agency (IRMA), a self-insurance group available only for Illinois municipalities. The girl's mother filed a negligence suit against Hillside. The village countered that it was immune from liability.

The court ruled that membership in the self-insurance group did not constitute a waiver of immunity by Hillside.

ISSUE. Illinois law provided that a municipality could protect itself from liability by the purchase of an insurance policy, which effectively then operated as a waiver of immunity. Does membership in a self-insurance group also constitute a waiver of immunity?

DECISION. The central issue to governmental immunity is whether tax revenues are being diverted from public functions. In the instance of self-insurance, a public entity bears all risks, and settlements are paid directly from governmental revenues; hence, there is not a waiver of immunity.

Self-insurance is distinguished from a commercial coverage because self-insurance can require supplemental contributions to cover liabilities and there are no private or non-governmental investors. The self-insurance concept allows small public entities to pool their resources and share the risks and costs of civil liabilities, and to protect themselves from potential fiscal disasters.

Municipal Limitations

Immunity protection for municipal functions and facilities has largely been abolished. Other than those few instances when the city, town, or village is clearly fulfilling a state function, municipalities rarely benefit from governmental immunity protection. Primary sources for determining whether a municipality is serving a state function are the state constitution, and the state legislature.[3] When the municipality is performing a function mandated by either source, it is a state function. However, municipal immunity cases rarely result from misinterpretation of a state law. More than likely, the case originates out of a misunderstanding relating to the daily operations of the municipal facility. In *Oien v. City of Sioux Falls*, the issue related to a municipal swimming pool; in *Maryland-National Capital Park and Planning Commission v. Kranz,* the court allowed that waiver of immunity applied to all functions.

The management of a municipal swimming pool is not protected by governmental immunity.

OIEN V. CITY OF SIOUX FALLS
393 N.W.2d 286
Supreme Court of South Dakota
September 10, 1986

FACTS. Municipal employees, who chemically treated the water at a municipal swimming pool, left a residue at the edge of the pool. A four-year-old girl sat down at the edge, came in contact with the chemicals, and was burned and scarred.

Her mother filed a lawsuit against the city of Sioux Falls alleging the municipality had been negligent in the operation of the pool. The court rejected the city's claim that it was protected by a South Dakota law which granted immunity to municipalities for the operation of their parks, playgrounds, and pools.

ISSUE. The South Dakota Constitution provides:

> "All courts shall be open, and every man for an injury done him in his property, person or reputation, shall have remedy be due course of law, and right and justice, administered without denial or delay." (Art. VI, 20)

How did the immunity statute conflict with this constitutional provision?

DECISION. A governmental function is an act discharged in the interest of the general public and protected by sovereign immunity. This immunity extends to municipalities when they act as a state agency. However, an administrative function that solely benefits the municipality is a *proprietary* function unprotected by sovereign immunity.

Unlike the United States Constitution, which was a "grant" of powers to the federal legislature, a state constitution serves as a "limitation" of powers upon the state legislature. So, the sovereign immunity article of the state constitution:

1. is not a "grant" to the state legislature to enact public pool immunity statutes to protect cities; and

2. the immunity statute violates the "open court" provision of the state constitution because pool management is a *proprietary* function, not a *governmental* function.

Sovereign immunity is not available to the Maryland State Park Commission.

MARYLAND-NATIONAL CAPITAL PARK AND PLANNING
COMMISSION V. KRANZ
521 A.2d 729
Court of Appeals of Maryland
March 3, 1987

FACTS. The plaintiff filed a suit for damages against the Maryland State Park Commission alleging that he was manhandled by a commission policeman, resulting in serious injury to his elbow. The commission, a state agency, was required by law to establish an insurance program to pay tort claims. Governmental immunity was extended only for claims based on malicious conduct, for punitive damages, or in excess of insurance limits.

The court rejected the commission's defense that it was a state agency protected by immunity for all of its functions.

ISSUE. The commission's immunity for tort actions was waived by the Maryland General Assembly's order to provide insurance coverage. Is the commission protected by immunity for any governmental functions?

DECISION. The court stated:

"As this court has often pointed out, the doctrine that the state of Maryland and state agencies are generally immune from suits, unless the immunity has been waived by the General Assembly is firmly entrenched in the law of Maryland. . . On the other hand, counties and municipalities do not possess this general immunity. Instead, counties and municipalities have never been given immunity in contract actions, and, in tort actions, they are not immune with regard to those matters categorized as 'proprietary' but are immune with regard to those matters categorized as governmental." (p. 731)

The legislature mandated that all claims based on tortious conduct were to be covered through an insurance program. The legislature did not intend that torts were to be classified according to their discretionary or proprietary function. Immunity for all tortious conduct, regardless of function, had been waived.

The court also ruled that the distinction between the terms "sovereign immunity" and "governmental immunity" is illusory, as the terms are used interchangeably.

GOVERNMENTAL IMMUNITY

Governmental immunity protects public agencies for their discretionary functions. A discretionary function relates to high-level, decision-making policy that usually is mandated or authorized by the state law. A public agency's proprietary functions are not protected by immunity. These are not decision-making in nature; rather, they refer to the necessary conduct to execute or carry out the duties of the discretionary function.[4]

Understanding Discretionary Functions

Discretionary functions have broad application to any duties or conduct authorized by the state legislature. For example, this chapter examines the day-to-day management of a recreational park area in relation to functions protected by immunity. Generally, a public agency (e.g., the Department of Natural Resources) charged with the duty of establishing parks is protected by immunity. Therefore, it would be immune from liability resulting from its decisions of where and when to build the park, how it was to be staffed, and how it would be equipped.

However, does immunity protect the park from the claim of a user who is injured as the result of the poor maintenance or supervision of the park? Are operations of the park which generate revenues or profits, or charge user fees (*Koh v. Village Green of Woodridge*) protected functions too? Is the government's decision to permit private rafting operations on its waterways protected by immunity as in *King v. United States Forest Service*?

Illinois Tort immunity protection is applied to public golf courses.

KOH V. VILLAGE GREENS OF WOODRIDGE
511 N.E.2d 854
Appellate Court of Illinois, 2nd Dist.
July 23, 1987

FACTS. The plaintiff was playing in a golf tournament at a public course operated by the Village of Woodridge, Illinois. She was a member of a foursome waiting to tee off at the first tee when she was struck by a golf ball hit by another participant in the tournament.

The plaintiff filed a damage suit against the village for her injuries. She alleged the village failed to properly manage the crowd at the first tee and that she was placed in a dangerous location while waiting to tee off. However, the court dismissed her case citing that the village was immune from liability under the Tort Immunity Act.

ISSUE. The Tort Immunity Act states:

"Neither a local public entity nor a public employee is liable for an injury caused by a failure to supervise an activity on or the use of any public property." (p. 855)

Though the Tort Immunity Act would apply to the village's *failure* to supervise the tournament, does it apply when the village apparently has voluntarily undertaken supervision? Does the Tort Immunity Act apply if the plaintiff paid a fee to use the golf course?

DECISION. The voluntary undertaking of duties of supervision for the golf tournament did not affect the village's tort immunity protection. The court would not distinguish the "failure" to supervise from alleged deficiencies in the supervision once it was undertaken.

The court referred to the payment of user fees for the public course as a "nominal fee," insufficient to exclude the village from immunity protection.

United States Forest Service is immune from liability for granting management permits to private rafting expeditions.

KING V. UNITED STATES FOREST SERVICE
647 F. Supp. 20
United States District Court, N.D. California
May 30, 1986

FACTS. The decedent drowned on a rafting expedition on the Yuba River in California. The expedition, under the direction of the White Water West Company, was operating under a permit granted by the United States Forest Service. The decedent's widow sued the Forest Service alleging, under the Federal Tort Claims Act, the Forest Service failed to regulate White Water West properly, failed to warn the plaintiff of the dangers of unusually high water, and misrepresented the safety of the trip.

The court dismissed the suit ruling that the supervision of activities, or the failure thereof, by the defendant was a discretionary function.

ISSUE. A discretionary function means:

"When an agency determines the extent to which it will supervise the safety procedures of private individuals, it is exercising discretionary regulatory authority of the most basic kind." (p. 21)

The Federal Tort Claims Act permits certain types of lawsuits to be filed against the government. A discretionary function is protected by governmental immunity, and is an exception to the Federal Tort Claims Act. Is the Forest Service immune from liability, or does it have a duty of care to the rafters under the Federal Tort Claims Act?

DECISION. The discretionary function rule exempts federal agencies from liability for their regulatory decision-making.

In this case, the court ruled that governmental decisions to warn, or not to warn, of dangers have traditionally been considered discrete roles based on policy decisions, and fall within the immunity protection.

The decision not to supervise the White Water West group is also considered a discretionary function. The adopted policy of the Forest Service regarding the issuance of permits had been followed, per the guidelines of its handbook; therefore, the court refused "to go behind the defendant's policy judgment and determine how permittees (White Water West) should have been regulated."

Understanding Management Functions

Many jurisdictions refuse to treat state law with such a broad brush. They limit the scope of discretionary functions. For example, the day-to-day management and operations of swimming facilities were not considered protected government activities in *Avallone v. Board of County Commissioners of Citrus County* and *Richardson v. Jackson County*.

Governmental immunity was applied to decision-making functions, not the daily operations of a public swimming area.

AVALLONE V. BOARD OF COUNTY COMMISSIONERS OF CITRUS COUNTY
497 So.2d 934
District Court of Appeal of Florida, 5th District
November 13, 1986

FACTS. The plaintiff was at a swimming area owned and operated by Citrus County (Florida). She was injured when a group of rowdies pushed her from a dock into the water. She filed a lawsuit against the county for its failure to provide supervisory personnel at the swimming area.

Citrus County asked for a dismissal of the case contending that it was protected by governmental immunity. The court ruled that issues regarding knowledge of the roughhousing, the potential for injury to patrons, and the failure to provide supervisory personnel were properly determined by a jury, not the court.

ISSUE. The Doctrine of Sovereign Immunity provides that discretionary, planning-level decisions by governmental agencies are protected from tort liability. Is the decision whether or not to provide lifeguards or supervisory personnel a discretionary, planning level decision, protected by immunity?

DECISION. The law in Florida was:

> "A government unit has the discretionary authority to operate or not to operate swimming facilities and is immune from suit on that discretionary question. However, once the unit decides to operate the swimming facility, it assumes the common law duty to operate the facility safely, just as a private individual is obligated under like circumstances." (p. 935)

Therefore, the Florida District Court of Appeal ruled Citrus County was not protected by immunity.

County swimming facility is not immune from liability for its failure to provide proper placement of swimming buoys.

RICHARDSON V. JACKSON COUNTY
407 N.W.2d 74
Court of Appeals of Michigan
May 4, 1987

FACTS. The decedent, a non-swimmer, drowned at Vandercook Lake, a park operated by Jackson County (Michigan). The swimming area was marked with buoys. However, the county failed to obtain the permits required for their proper placement as required by the Michigan Marine Safety Act.

The county maintained that the operation of the park was a governmental function protected by immunity. The court disagreed and refused the county's request for dismissal of the lawsuit filed by the decedent's heirs.

ISSUE. A governmental function, which is protected by immunity, is an activity "expressly or impliedly mandated or authorized by constitution, statute, or other law."

Michigan law provides that operation and maintenance of a park is a governmental function. The county contended the issue in this case was its negligent failure to properly place the swimming buoys; further, it enjoyed immunity, regardless of whether its actions were negligent or not.

DECISION. The court ruled that the precise issue was not operation of a park; rather, it was the operation of a swimming area subject to the requirements of the Marine Safety Act. In that sense, the failure to obtain the permits was illegal (not merely negligent). The precise function (operation of the swimming area) was not a protected governmental function.

NOTE: Is the commission of an act, as opposed to the omission of an act, required for the application of governmental immunity?

The court maintained that the commission of the act was required. Therefore, had the court solely focused on the issue of park operation (rather than operation of the swimming area as a component part of the overall park operations), the county would have been protected by immunity.

Exceptions to Immunity

In some jurisdictions, the care and custody of real estate is treated as an exception to governmental immunity. For example, Pennsylvania has a Real Property Exception to its governmental immunity law. However, there are two difficult questions when dealing with real property exceptions: is personal property and equipment included in the exception, and how are supervisory duties distinguished from the care of property? In *McNeill by McNeill*, which follows, the court distinguished property maintenance from supervision under the Real Property Exception.

A Pennsylvania city park is neither protected by governmental immunity, nor by limited immunity of the recreational use statute.

McNEILL BY McNEILL V. CITY OF PHILADELPHIA
522 A.2d 174
Commonwealth Court of Pennsylvania
March 11, 1987

FACTS. A 10-year-old boy was injured when he struck a thin wire supporting a tennis court net while riding his bicycle in a Philadelphia city park. His father filed a negligence suit against the city. The court, over the city's objection that it was protected by governmental immunity, sent the case back for a new trial to determine if the state's real property exception to governmental immunity, or the recreational use law, applied to the case.

ISSUE. What is the real property exception to governmental immunity? The Recreation Use Act limits the liability of landowners who allow persons to enter their property for recreational purposes without fee. Is that Act applicable to this case?

DECISION. The focus of the real property exception is the maintenance of property, not the supervision of employees and children. The father argued that his claim was based on the city's negligent care of the park, not its negligent supervision of his child.

The Recreation Act is interpreted to apply to large, private, and primarily unimproved lands used for outdoor recreation by the general public for no fee. The type of recreational equipment would be of a type used in open spaces, not enclosed, urban recreational facilities. Therefore, there were also genuine issues whether or not the park was an area protected by the Recreation Act.

But, in *Kasavage v. City of Philadelphia*, the court stated that the Real Property Exception applied only when the injury resulted from a condition or defect in the property.

Pennsylvania's Real Property Exception to governmental immunity relates to park conditions, not the supervision of children.

KASAVAGE V. CITY OF PHILADELPHIA
524 A.2d 1089
Commonwealth Court of Pennsylvania
May 1, 1987

FACTS. The court recited the facts in this case as:

> "(The parents) instituted an action against the City for injuries suffered by Stanley Kasavage at the City's Cione Playground and Pool. The complaint alleged that on July 6, 1984, Stanley was injured at the pool, suffering a lacerated and fractured nose, by a group of rowdy juveniles the City failed to control. (The parents) complain that the City knew or should have known of the dangerous activities at the pool and that it was negligent in failing to supervise the area, in permitting a dangerous condition to develop and in failing to warn pool patrons of the dangerous conditions." (p. 1090)

The case was dismissed because the city was protected by governmental immunity.

ISSUE. Generally, a Pennsylvania municipality is not liable for damages for injuries caused by the acts of any city agency or employee. There are, however, eight exceptions to the immunity protection, including the following:

> "Real Property - The care, custody or control of real property in the possession of the local agency, except that the local agency shall not be liable for damages on account of any injury sustained by a person intentionally trespassing on real property in the possession of the local agency." (p. 1090)

Does the real property exception apply to this case?

DECISION. The court ruled that the activity leading to the youngster's injury did not involve the care, custody, or control of the pool. The cause of the injury was the city's failure to supervise disruptive juveniles.

The failure to supervise was conduct unrelated to the Real Property Exception; therefore, the city was protected by governmental immunity.

In order to fall within the Exception:

> "The conduct complained of must be directly related to the condition of the premises, . . . or an injury must result from some defect in the real estate." (p. 1091)

RECREATIONAL USE IMMUNITY

The purpose of recreational use laws is to relieve landowners from any liability for injuries occurring to recreational users of their property. The common characteristics of recreational use statutes are:

1. The landowner may not charge a fee for the recreational use of the land.

2. The landowner does not owe a duty to inspect, repair, or maintain the premises for its safe use.

3. The landowner enjoys immunity for his or her negligent conduct.

4. Recreational uses usually are outdoor activities such as fishing, hunting, camping, boating, and swimming.

The application of recreational use law primarily depends on whether a fee has been charged for use of the property. If no fee has been charged, the landowner is not liable for injuries arising as a result of his or her negligence. When a fee is charged, the landowner owes the user the affirmative duty of care to maintain the premises, to repair any defects, and to warn of dangerous or hazardous conditions.

The limited immunity of recreational use law is predicated on the negligent conduct of the landowner. Any acts by the landowner constituting wilful, wanton, or reckless misconduct are not protected by recreational use protection.

The original intent of recreational use legislation was to provide a limited protection for private landowners, but the courts in many states have not been reluctant to apply limited protection to publicly-owned lands as well. In *Page v. City of Louisville*, recreational use immunity was applied as an alternative to governmental immunity; in *Jenkinson v. Department of Natural Resources*, recreational use immunity was applicable with governmental immunity; and in *O'Neal v. United States*, Oregon's recreational use immunity was applied to federal lands. Thus, public agencies wield a double-edged sword: governmental immunity for decision-making functions, and limited immunity for recreational use applications.

A public park facility is not liable for its negligence under Kentucky recreational use law.

PAGE V. CITY OF LOUISVILLE
722 S.W.2d 60
Court of Appeals of Kentucky
December 24, 1986

FACTS. The plaintiff was injured when he stepped into a hole at Iroquois Park, a facility operated by the Metropolitan Parks and Recreation Board (Louisville), a joint city-county agency. His negligence suit was dismissed by the court under recreational use immunity protection.

ISSUE. What duties of care, if any, were owed to the plaintiff by the defendant? How did recreational use immunity apply to this case?

DECISION. Due to the complex structure of the joint city-county agency, the Kentucky Court of Appeals did not review whether there were any governmental immunity defenses available to the defendant.

Instead, the Court applied a recreational use statute which stated:

> "... that an owner of land, who makes it available to the public for recreational purposes without payment of fees, is under no general duty and a person entering upon the premises takes the land as he finds it to be." (p. 61)

On that basis, absent any wilful or malicious behavior by the city-county agency, the city of Louisville was not liable.

A state park operated by the Michigan Department of Natural Resources is protected by governmental immunity and recreational use immunity.

JENKINSON V. DEPARTMENT OF NATURAL RESOURCES
406 N.W.2d 302
Court of Appeals of Michigan
April 20, 1987

FACTS. The decedent drowned while wading at the Bald Mountain State Recreation Area operated by the Michigan Department of Natural Resources (DNR). The decedent's heirs filed a lawsuit alleging his death was caused by the DNR's negligence.

The court dismissed the suit ruling the claim was barred by governmental immunity, *and* by Michigan's recreational use law.

ISSUE. Is the management of a swimming beach a park management function protected by governmental immunity?

DECISION. The court ruled that the operation of the recreation area was expressly authorized by state statute; therefore, it was protected by immunity as a governmental function.

Michigan's recreational use statute is applicable to its publicly-owned lands. Since the case was a negligence claim, not an action for wilful and wanton misconduct on the part of the DNR, the suit was also barred by the recreational use law.

NOTE: Is there a functional difference between establishing park facilities and the management of the park facilities?

Oregon recreational use immunity protects the federal government from claims by recreational users.

O'NEAL V. UNITED STATES
814 F.2d 1285
United States Court of Appeals, 9th Circuit
February 19, 1987

FACTS. A husband and wife, hunting bear in Oregon, were injured when their motor vehicle slid off a road into a creek. The accident occurred on lands maintained by the United States Bureau of Land Management.

Their lawsuit against the United States for its negligence in the construction, maintenance, and management of the road was dismissed. The court ruled that Oregon's recreation use statute applied to the United States as a landowner, and exempted the government from liability.

ISSUE. The Oregon law provided that, absent reckless conduct, a landowner is exempt from liability for injuries suffered by a user who is using the land for recreational purposes for no fee. Does a state law, intended for private landowners, apply to federal lands as well?

DECISION. Under the Federal Tort Claims Act:

"The United States shall be liable, respecting the provisions of this title relating to tort claims, in the same manner and to the same extent as a private individual under like circumstances.."

A lawsuit against the government under the Federal Tort Claims Act is decided on the same state law that a private suit would be judged. The Oregon recreational use law applied to federally-owned property; thus, the government was protected by immunity.

Fees

Recreational use immunity will not apply when a fee is charged for the recreational use of the real estate. However, since a number of states apply recreational use statutes to publicly-owned lands, the courts are having to distinguish whether facility entry fees constitute prohibited charges. In *Schiller v. Muskegon State Park*, recreational use immunity was not limited by the payment of a park entry fee.

The payment of a park entry fee does not affect the application of Michigan's recreational use act.

SCHILLER V. MUSKEGON STATE PARK
395 N.W.2d 75
Court of Appeals of Michigan
July 21, 1986

FACTS. The plaintiff was injured unloading a boat at a boat launch at Muskegon State Park (Michigan). He filed a lawsuit alleging the boat dock was slippery and wet; that the dock constituted an unreasonable risk of harm to people using it; and that the defendants had failed to inspect the dock, warn of its dangers, or otherwise exercise due diligence.

At the time of the accident, the Michigan Recreational Use Act provided that landowners were not liable to recreational users of their property who did not pay "valuable consideration" for that use. The plaintiff contended that the Recreation Use Act did not apply since he paid for a park permit to enter the park. The court disagreed and dismissed his case.

ISSUE. Does payment of the entry fee constitute valuable consideration?

DECISION. The court cited prior Michigan decisions which applied the protection of the Recreational Use Act to state-owned parks.

The permit fee authorized the entry of motor vehicles to the park and was for use of the roads and parking lots therein. The state had the right to require additional permit fees for bikes, horses, and walking. As such, the permit fee paid by the plaintiff did not constitute valuable consideration.

In *Hogue v. Stone Mountain Memorial Association*, the combination of parking fees, camping fees, and concession charges did not stop the court from applying recreational use immunity.

Parking permit fees, camping fees, concessions and amusement fees at Stone Mountain Park (Georgia) are not charges excluding the park from the immunity protection of the recreational property act.

HOGUE V. STONE MOUNTAIN MEMORIAL ASSOCIATION
358 S.E.2d 852
Court of Appeals of Georgia
May 29, 1987

FACTS. The plaintiff and her family were camping at Stone Mountain Park, Georgia. The family paid a $4.00 vehicle entry fee, paid a camping fee, and spent money at the park concessions and rides. On the last night of their stay, the family was walking to a laser light show when the plaintiff stepped off a ledge and fractured her ankle.

The court dismissed her negligence lawsuit, ruling that it was barred by Georgia's Recreational Property Act.

ISSUE. Under the Georgia Recreational Property Act, a landowner is not liable for the negligent injuries to recreational users who are on the land at the landowner's invitation or permission *without charge*. Are the parking fees, camping fees, and concession costs *charges* within the meaning of the act? Should the court have applied the recreation use act?

DECISION. The court distinguished the prohibited charges from the fees which were paid. The parking fee was a permit for vehicle entrance only, not recreational use; and the other fees were not considered for recreational use since activities such as swimming and sightseeing were available without charge.

Stone Mountain Park was established by state law as a "public recreational area" notwithstanding the fact that substantial revenues were derived from permits, concessions, and ride fees. Since the injuries occurred as a result of a recreational use for which no fee was charged, the provisions of the act were applicable.

NOTE: There was a dissenting opinion to this ruling which agreed there was recreational use derived from a visit to the park, but questioned whether the public invitation did not further the "business" interests of the park.

Expanding Recreational Uses

Recreational use laws generally define the recreational activities protected by the limited immunity. The early history of most statutes reveals that the protected activities were limited to those occurring in the "great outdoors," such as hunting and fishing. In time, boating, swimming, and other recreational waterway activities were added. Today, most statutes also contain a catch-all clause to incorporate any other recognized "recreational" activity.

With the application of recreational use law to public lands, the types of protected activities expanded from those largely identified with outdoor, undeveloped lands to park swings in urban parks (*McGhee v. City of Glenns Ferry*), to urban bicycling and jogging paths (*Riksem v. City of Seattle*), and to private homes (*Wright v. Dudley*).

A municipality is not liable for the injury suffered by a child playing on a swing in a city park.

McGHEE V. CITY OF GLENNS FERRY
729 P.2d 396
Supreme Court of Idaho
November 26, 1986

FACTS. A young girl fell from a swing in a city park operated and maintained by the city of Glenns Ferry (Idaho). Her mother filed a negligence action which the court dismissed on the basis of recreational immunity. The court cited the Idaho law which limited the liability of landowners who allowed users on their land for recreational purposes without charge.

The court rejected the mother's argument that the statute did not apply to a city or that the operation and maintenance of a city park fell outside the scope of "recreational purposes."

ISSUE. What is the basis for application of the recreational use law?

DECISION. The court reviewed the intent of the legislature when the statute was enacted. The court based its decision on "what is said in the statute, and we will construe statutory terms according to their plain, obvious, and rational meanings."

Accordingly, the court did not distinguish the operation and maintenance of the park for recreational purposes from the "inducement" afforded private landowners. The court said that Glenns Ferry was owner of the public property and that the Idaho law applied to public property. Additionally, the court ruled the park swing was a recreational activity, and within the meaning of the statute.

Washington's recreational immunity extends to commuters as well as recreational users of Seattle city parks.

RIKSEM V. CITY OF SEATTLE
736 P.2d 275
Court of Appeals of Washington, Div. 1
February 23, 1987

FACTS. A bicyclist, riding on a multi-use trail maintained by the city of Seattle, collided with a jogger. The cyclist sued the city for damages resulting from his injury, alleging negligent *and* reckless conduct by the city in maintaining the trail, and failing to provide adequate warnings and traffic control.

The court dismissed the case ruling that the city was immune from liability under Washington's Recreational Use Statute.

ISSUE. The Recreational Use Statute provides that landowners, *public or private*, are not liable for unintentional injuries to recreational users who are on their lands at no charge. The purpose of the law is to limit the liability of landowners, and provide an impetus for public recreational use.

The plaintiff alleged that the statute violated the equal protection clause of the federal and state constitutions, since persons who were traversing the lands strictly for commuting or non-recreational uses would have the right to sue landowners for injuries and recreational users would not.

DECISION. The Recreational Use Statute applies equally to recreational users or to persons just traversing the land for commuting purpose. The court reasoned that commuters were gaining secondary recreational benefits by walking or biking. Further, recreational use statutes should not be strictly construed so as to exempt incidental recreational uses from their coverage.

Michigan recreational land use statute applies to invited guests injured in the backyard of their host.

WRIGHT V. DUDLEY
404 N.W.2d 217
Court of Appeals of Michigan
December 22, 1986

FACTS. A youngster, socializing with a group of friends at the defendant's home, dove from a dock extending from the defendant's backyard into Clear Lake (Michigan). The water was only three feet deep; the youth broke his neck when his head hit the bottom.

His mother filed a lawsuit against the defendant to recover damages for the resulting paralysis. The court dismissed the case ruling that the defendant was immune from liability under Michigan Recreational Land Use Act.

ISSUE. The Michigan law provides:

> "No cause of action shall arise for injuries to any person who is on the lands of another without paying to such other person a valuable consideration for the purpose of fishing, hunting, trapping, camping, hiking, sightseeing, motorcycling, snowmobiling, or any other outdoor recreational use, with or without permission, against the owner, tenant, or lessee of said premises unless the injuries were caused by the gross negligence or wilful and wanton misconduct of the owner, tenant, or lessee"(p. 217-218)

DECISION. The youngster's mother argued that the recreation use statute did not apply to social guests who are injured in the backyard of their host. The court, however, stated that the language of the statute was unambiguous and plain; the language did not suggest any other application. The statute clearly applied to persons using the land of others for recreational purposes.

The court further ruled that the failure to provide warnings, barriers, buoys, or lifeguards did not constitute wilful and wanton misconduct. Wilful and wanton misconduct "is made out only if the conduct alleged shows an intent to harm, or, if not that, such indifference to whether harm will result as to be the equivalent of a willingness that it does."

Inducement or Encouragement

A number of courts have rejected expanding recreational uses to include urban parks and social guests. Those courts have formulated two different tests for determining the applicability of recreational use law. Some courts concentrate on the nature of the recreational area itself to determine if it "encourages" recreational use? If recreational use is encouraged, the courts will not apply recreational immunity since the law is only intended to induce landowners to allow or permit recreational use of their property. The courts reason that when the inherent purpose of the recreational area encourages recreational use of its facilities, such as urban parks, then the appropriate affirmative duties of care should be required of the recreational facility.

A city is liable when its negligence causes injury to a bicyclist using its parks.

FERRES V. CITY OF NEW ROCHELLE
502 N.E.2d 972
Court of Appeals of New York
November 25, 1986

FACTS. The plaintiff rode his bicycle into a chain placed across the entrance to a municipal park operated by the city of New Rochelle. He filed a suit against New Rochelle alleging the city was negligent in placing the chain across the park entrance, and in failing to give adequate notice of the hazardous condition.

The court rejected the city's claim that the case was barred by New York's recreational use law.

ISSUE. New York law provides that a landowner owes no duty to keep his premises safe for entry or use, and is not obligated to give notice of hazardous conditions. The law does not absolve the owner of the premises for wilful or malicious acts. Should the law apply to public agencies that operate city parks?

DECISION. The controlling principle in the construction of a law is the legislative intent. Here, the legislative intent of the New York law was to provide owners an "inducement" to allow persons to use their property for recreational activities. The law assumed that, had an owner not been provided that inducement, the injured party would not have been permitted on the property in the first place.

The law does not apply to city parks maintained for recreational use by a general public which is "encouraged" to use them. Therefore, the city of New Rochelle is not immune from liability.

Other courts use a different standard. Recreational use immunity protection is applied only to large, undeveloped tracts of real estate, not urban parks or subdivided properties.[5]

Louisiana's recreational use law applied to rural or semi-rural land, not city park playgrounds.

HERBERT V. CITY OF KENNER
501 So.2d 901
Court of Appeal of Louisiana, 5th District
January 12, 1987

FACTS. A minor child, playing in the Susan Park Playground (Louisiana) with other children, was struck in the eye with mud thrown by one of his playmates. The youngster suffered permanent head and eye injuries. His father filed a lawsuit against the playmate's father.

The playmate's father and his insurance carrier then sued the city of Kenner, which operated and maintained the park. The court ruled the city of Kenner was not protected by immunity under the Louisiana Recreational Use Act.

ISSUE. The Louisiana law provides that owners who permit persons to use their lands for recreational purposes, *with or without charge*, are not liable for any injury to the users of the land, except for an owner's wilful and malicious failure to warn against "dangerous condition, use, structure, or activity . . ."

It is undisputed that the city of Kenner did not act wilfully or maliciously. Why is the city not protected by recreational use immunity?

DECISION. The court distinguished Louisiana's recreational use law ruling that it applied to rural and semi-rural lands: "suggestive of open and undeveloped expanses of property." The instrumentality causing the injury (in this case, mud) should be one encountered in the great outdoors, not available in a backyard. Therefore, the Court refused to apply the immunity protection of the statute.

NOTE: It is significant that the type of land and the instrument causing the injury were distinguishing factors in the application of the law. Other factors considered by many courts are whether the facilities are "open" or "encouraged" for public use.

Warnings

Landowners do not bear the responsibility for warning recreational users of dangerous conditions on the property. However, many of the cases challenging recreational use protection attempt to impose some duty for conditional warnings, as in *Addessi v. Connecticut Light and Power Company* and *Stuart v. City of Morgan City.*[6]

Recreational use statutes do not require posted warnings.

ADDESSI V. CONNECTICUT LIGHT AND POWER CO.
521 A.2d 605
Appellate Court of Connecticut
March 3, 1987

FACTS. The plaintiff was injured when he dove from a dock into Candlewood Lake, owned by Connecticut Light and Power Co.(CL&P). His negligence action was dismissed because CL&P was immune from liability under Connecticut law which provided, in part:

"General Statutes Sec. 52-577g does not purport to prohibit or regulate conduct, but to relieve under appropriate circumstances an owner of recreational land from liability to others who use its land for recreational purposes." (p. 606)

ISSUE. The plaintiff argued the law was vague. Specifically, he contended that a person of ordinary intelligence would not understand what conduct was prohibited by the statute, and that the statute should require landowners to post warnings that they are immune from liability for recreational injuries occurring on their properties.

DECISION. A suit based on vagueness must address itself to the language contained in the statute, not what is omitted. The legislature could have required that owners post warnings as a requirement for protection under the statute; however, the statute is not void because the legislature chose not to require such warnings.

A diver is responsible to determine the danger of a dive.

STUART V. CITY OF MORGAN CITY
504 So.2d 934
Court of Appeal of Louisiana, 1st Circuit
March 4, 1987

FACTS. The plaintiff entered the municipal park at Lake Palourde (Louisiana) at 2:30 a.m., through open gates. He dived into the lake from a stack of sand bags located at the edge of the shore. The water was shallow. The plaintiff struck his head on the bottom, severed his spine, and was rendered quadriplegic.

He filed a negligence action against the city, parish, and state governments for their failure to warn of a dangerous condition. The court dismissed the case, ruling there was no duty to warn him of any dangers under the recreational use law.

ISSUE. Louisiana's recreational use law provided that a landowner did not owe recreational users on his land a duty to keep the premises safe, or to warn of known dangers.

DECISION. The focus of the Louisiana law is that a landowner "owes no duty of care" and "cannot incur liability." There is neither a duty of care under a negligence theory, nor is there a duty for the higher degree of care required by dangerous conditions.

The purpose of the recreational use law was to relieve landowners, including governmental units, from liability. To impose a duty on those same landowners to post danger warnings would defeat the purpose of the recreational use law.

A diver is primarily responsible for determining the danger of a dive. The plaintiff previously had made dives into this particular lake, and could have determined the depth of the water by walking out a few feet from the water's edge.

STATUTORY INTENT—THE FLOOD CONTROL ACT OF 1928

Courts are required to interpret and apply statutes according to their plain, unambiguous, and clear language, and with an understanding of the legislative intent behind the enactment of the statute. It is important to understand that the original language of immunity statutes may not necessarily evoke the foresight, or lack of foresight, of the legislators who passed the laws. For example, there have been a number of cases involving the application of the Flood Control Act of 1928.

The Flood Control Act of 1928 provided the government with immunity for its part in the building and maintenance of flood control projects after catastrophic flooding along the Mississippi River in 1927. As the flood control projects gradually came under control of the Army Corps of Engineers, the immunity was understood to apply to any function of flood control, regardless of negligence or wilful and wanton misconduct.

As time passed, however, the government started to promote many flood control projects for recreational waterway uses. Whether or not those uses could be foreseen by the legislators who passed the Flood Control Act, or whether or not those legislators intended for the immunity to expand to unforeseen recreational uses remains in doubt. Today, the use of recreational waterways located on flood control projects remains an "at-your-own risk" activity according to the language of the Flood Control Act of 1928.

The United States is protected from liability for its management of recreational waterways on flood control projects.

UNITED STATES V. JAMES
106 S.Ct 3116
United States Supreme Court
July 2, 1986

FACTS. This case involved two negligence claims against the Army Corps of Engineers which opened flood gates, without warning, on Arkansas and Louisiana reservoirs.

In the Arkansas case, the gates were opened, and two water skiers became caught in the current. The husband of one skier dove into the water in an attempt to save them, but he drowned with the other skier, while his wife was severely injured.

In the Louisiana case, a father and son's fishing boat was swept to the flood gates which had been opened. The son drowned when he was pulled through a 220-foot drainage barrel.

In both lawsuits, the court ruled the government was immune from liability under the provisions of the Flood Control Act of 1928, despite finding in the Arkansas case that the government had wilfully and maliciously failed to warn of the danger; in the Louisiana case, the government had negligently failed to warn of the danger.

ISSUE. The Flood Control Act of 1928 states that the government is not liable for any damage, for any reason, resulting from its management of flood control waterways.

DECISION. According to the court, the legislative history of the Act showed that congressional intent was to grant immunity to the government for its assumption of flood control projects along the Mississippi River after catastrophic flooding in 1927.

The Army Corps of Engineers' failure to warn of the opened flood gates was considered part of the management function protected by immunity.

REFERENCES

Davis, K.C. 1972. *Administrative Law Text*. 3rd ed., 466-484. St. Paul, MN: West Publishing Co.

Kionka, E. 1977. *Torts: Injuries to Perons and Property*. Nutshell Series: 398-421. St. Paul, MN: West Publishing Co.

Prosser, W. 1984. *The Law of Torts*. W.P. Keeton 5th ed., 1032-1075. St. Paul, MN: West Publishing Co.

[1] Wilful and wanton misconduct was distinguished in the *Jacobs* case reported in Chapter One. The misconduct was easily identified due to the theater's disregard of previous accidents, its failure to provide proper lighting, and its lack of supervision relating to warning procedures. *Jacobs v. Commonwealth Highland Theatres, Inc.* 738 P.2d 6 (Colo. Ct. App. 1986).

[2] In *Overcash v. Statesville City Board of Education*, 348 S.E.2d 524 (N.C. Ct. App. 1986), a school board immunity was waived only to the extent of the policy limits of its liability policy for an injury claim filed by a high school baseball player. In *Nelson v. House*, 402 N.W.2d 639 (Minn. Ct. App. 1987), the court ruled that an injured cheerleader's claim was limited to the liability limits set by state law, regardless of her actual damages.

[3] Public schools and universities are considered state agencies because their governing authority is vested by the state legislature.

[4] The supervisory duties of a physical education teacher were considered "ministerial" acts in *Hyman v. Green*, 403 N.W.2d 597 (Mich. Ct. App. 1987). When the teacher failed to carry out his supervisory duties resulting in a student's injury, the court ruled the teacher was not immune from liability since ministerial acts are not protected under governmental immunity.

[5] The Michigan Supreme Court traced the history of the Michigan Recreational Land Use Act in *Wymer v. Holmes*, 412 N.W.2d 213 (Mich. 1987). It ruled that swimming accidents occurring at urban homes or on subdivided real estate were not recreational activities protected by immunity. This case was decided only nine months after the Michigan Court of Appeals ruled that the recreational use law protected a landowner from liability for a swimming accident occurring in his backyard.

[6] The Washington State Recreation Use Act, which includes publicly-owned lands within its protection, does require conspicuous warning signs for latent artificial conditions. *Preston by Preston v. Pierce County*, 741 P.2d 71 (Wash. Ct. App. 1987).

Chapter 3

Physical Education Issues

INTRODUCTION

This chapter examines the legal role of supervision in physical education. Though neither a new, nor a unique topic to physical education law, supervision is rapidly developing a separate meaning under the law than it has in practice for the physical educator. Supervision is recognized as one of many functions required of the physical educator. The inspection and distribution of equipment is another. However, the legal liability attached to these two duties is not always the same. Many states protect educators from liability for supervisory functions under the immunity theory of *in loco parentis* status. (That legal concept provides that educators stand as parents to their students with all parental rights, responsibilities, and privileges.) The same educators, however, may be liable for furnishing, or failing to furnish, equipment to students. From the practical point of view of the educator, it may be easy to distinguish supervisory duties from equipment care and control. From the legal point of view, it is increasingly difficult to differentiate those functions.

We should first understand the precarious place physical education holds in the world of educational liabilities. The age and maturity of school children, as well as the inherently risky nature of physical activity, requires a great degree of care by the physical educator; that degree of care may require more of the physical education teacher than other educators for a number of reasons.

First, the physical educator supervises many potentially dangerous activities not performed in a classroom. Second, the physical educator teaches and supervises those functions in facilities which present their own unique risks, again separate from the classroom. Finally, the instruction, direction, and guidance required of physical educators includes requisite instruction of motor skills for immature bodies, as well as minds.

SUPERVISION

Much of the recent case law in physical education issues revolves around the supervisory role of the teacher. The potential liabilities of supervision originate with the legal authority held by educators. Historically, educators have enjoyed *in loco parentis* status;[1] that is, in matters relating to student discipline and school control, during school hours teachers enjoy the same privileges of authority as parents. In most jurisdictions, that authority includes the right to inflict corporal punishment for student's misbehavior. However, the infliction of corporal punishment is usually only permitted for the breach of reasonable school rules.

The teacher's authority is limited to school functions on the school premises, during school hours. Although the courts are sometimes protective of teachers for imposing student discipline after school hours, educators should be cautious to insure that any student misconduct has a direct bearing on the well-being of the school before imposing their authority.

The rule of the "reasonable man" is still the test by which liability is adjudicated. Understanding that physical educators may owe a greater duty of care because of the immaturity of their subjects and the potential danger of the activites, the basis for imposing liability remains: what would a person of comparable training, skills, and expertise have done under similar circumstances?

A teacher can require a male student to perform disciplinary push-ups in the nude in the boys' locker room.

JACKSON V. CITY OF WOOSTER BOARD OF EDUCATION
504 N.E.2d 1144
Court of Appeals of Ohio, Wayne Co.
November 20, 1985

FACTS. An eighth-grade student at Edgewood Junior High School (Wooster, Ohio), showered at the end of physical education class. He took two towels instead of the required one towel to dry off. When he refused to return one towel, he was directed by his physical education teacher to do 25 push-ups. The student's request to return to his locker to first put on his underwear was denied. He did the discipline in the nude.

The boy's parents filed a lawsuit against the teacher and the school alleging the negligent and/or intentional infliction of emotional distress upon their son. The suit was dismissed because the teacher's conduct was not outrageous, was not intended to cause the boy emotional distress, and did not result in serious emotional stress.

ISSUE. Ohio law awards damages for the intentional infliction of emotional distress, without an accompanying physical injury, under the following circumstances: the person causing the distress knew or should have known that serious emotional distress would result, the conduct goes beyond all bounds of decency, the actions are the proximate cause of emotional injury, and the mental anguish is so great that no reasonable person should be expected to endure it.

DECISION. It was evident to the court that the teacher's actions were intended to ensure quick and certain discipline, and not to emotionally injure the youngster. At the time, the teacher was supervising 25 boys in what the court described as, "semi-organized chaos of a high school boys' locker room." Therefore, it was not outrageous conduct to require the push-ups in the nude. Otherwise, the student might beat a "hasty retreat through the bustle of the locker room." The evidence of actual emotional distress suffered by the student was inconclusive.

Physical educators owe their students the duty to exercise the same ordinary and prudent care that a person of comparable skill and training would provide. Because of this, courts usually begin their analysis of legal liability with the supervisory role itself. Since the implicit duty of care includes an awareness that the subjects are children, that the activities may involve bodily risk, and that instruction and direction is generally provided outside the classroom, the greater degree of care can be formidable. Additionally, the physical educator must remain cognizant of any special student needs.

School district is not liable to a handicapped student injured from an exercise program designed by a state physical therapist.

GREENING V. SCHOOL DISTRICT OF MILLARD
393 N.W.2d 51
Supreme Court of Nebraska
September 5, 1986

FACTS. An 11-year-old student suffered from a congenital deformity known as Myelodysplasia. A common effect of Myelodysplasia was Osteoporosis, described as loss or diminishment of mineral in the bones, or "brittle bones."

A state-employed physical therapist designed an exercise program for the student which was performed in leg braces. The program was neither submitted for approval of a physician, nor discussed with school district supervisory personnel. The program was supervised by a school aide who was not a physical therapist, nor had any experience with Myelodysplasia.

During an exercise period, the student complained of pain in his right leg. The school aide decided to have the student continue the exercise anyway. That evening, it was discovered the student suffered a broken leg from the stress of the leg brace against the weakened bone.

The court dismissed the parent's lawsuit against the school as a result of the injury ruling that inadequate supervision was not the cause of the injury.

ISSUE. What were the duties of the school district, or the aide, to the student? Is the school district liable for an exercise program supervised by an aide unqualified and inexperienced in physical therapy?

DECISION. There was no evidence that the aide knew of the danger of the exercises. The school district relied on the competence of a state-qualified physical therapist. The school had no duty to verify the safety of the exercise program if it relied on the competence of a professional "trusted by the state with the responsibility of carrying out such a program."

The school district would be liable if the aide was incompetent *and* that the incompetency was the proximate cause of the injury. In this instance, the injury was caused by the therapist's defective program, not the aide's supervision of that program.

Regardless of the cause of the student's injury in the *Greening* case, do you think the school failed the student in its duty of care? The prudent physical educator should recognize that: if the school was not aware of the exercise plan, it should have been; if the school was not aware of the precise function of the aide, it should have been; and, if the aide was not aware of the nature of the student's pain, he should have been. The school should have recognized that the breakdown in communication, or lack of informative procedures, placed a helpless, handicapped student in great peril. In most cases, the school's awareness and communication procedures would have been the measure of ordinary, prudent care.

The traditional immunity protections afforded to schools and their personnel are changing. Even in the absence of state statutes, school personnel used to enjoy governmental immunity for the operation and management of the schools; although, even with those immunity protections, the courts distinguished and categorized supervisory functions, as in *Hyman v. Green*.

A physical education teacher is not immune from liability for the supervision of a physical education class.

HYMAN V. GREEN
403 N.W.2d 597
Court of Appeals of Michigan
February 3, 1987

FACTS. A freshman at West Bloomfield High School (Michigan) was injured while playing touch football during a first period physical education class. He filed a negligence suit against the physical education teacher for inadequate supervision of the class. Specifically, the student alleged the teacher was absent from the playing field, and was reading the morning paper when some of the players began to use excessive force which led to his injury.

There was no question by the parties that the school board was immune from liability due to governmental immunity. However, the court ruled the teacher did not enjoy the same immunity since his supervisory duties were "ministerial."

ISSUE. Shouldn't the teacher enjoy the same immunity protection as the school board?

DECISION. The court distinguished between teaching duties which are discretionary-decisional in nature and for which immunity is granted, and those duties which are ministerial in nature and for which immunity is not granted.

Decisions regarding the offering of the class, who will participate, and where and when to conduct the class are decision-making functions which are protected by governmental immunity. However, supervision of the class itself is a ministerial duty requiring minimal decision-making.

The court noted:

> "In the case at bar, we hold that a physical education instructor's supervision, or nonsupervision, of his students constitutes a ministerial act. Thus, where a student is injured because his instructor failed to adequately supervise the class, the instructor may be held liable in tort and the defense of governmental immunity is not available." (p. 598)

EQUIPMENT LIABILITIES

The purpose of this chapter is to clarify the legal distinction between the supervisory role and equipment role for physical educators. Many states distinguish those functions by separate duties of care. The physical educator may enjoy the protection of governmental immunity or *in loco parentis* status for supervisory functions. That immunity protection is only abrogated by an educator's wilful and wanton misconduct. However, the same jurisdictions might hold the educator to the ordinary, prudent duty of care when furnishing equipment to students. For example, in Pennsylvania, that duty is required by the Real Property Exception. But, in Illinois, furnishing unsafe equipment is recognized as a function separate from supervision. In both states, the equipment function imposes on the physical educator a duty of ordinary, prudent care for unprotected by in loco parentis immunity.

The Pennsylvania Real Property Exception

The Pennsylvania Real Property Exception to governmental immunity was briefly examined in Chapter Two. Its applicability to physical education issues only further highlights the limitations the courts are placing on previously protected supervisory duties. In *Cestari v. School District of Cheltenham Township* and *McCloskey v. Abington School District*, the courts distinguished supervisory duties from equipment provision. The decisions in those cases were important for two reasons. First, they represent the trend of the courts to include personal property or equipment within the "real" property concept. Second, they recognize that the duties of the physical educator include, in addition to inspection and fitting, the proper placement and installation of equipment.

The placement of landing mats for a pole vault pit is not a function protected by governmental immunity.

CESTARI V. SCHOOL DISTRICT OF CHELTENHAM TOWNSHIP
520 A.2d 110
Commonwealth Court of Pennsylvania
January 21, 1987

FACTS. A high school pole vaulter, competing in a track meet at Cheltenham High School (Pennsylvania), was injured when he failed to clear the pole. He landed with one foot on the landing mat, and one foot off the landing mat.

He filed a lawsuit alleging the school was negligent in its placement of mats and cushions and in the installation and maintenance of the pole vault pit. The court ruled the school was liable for its negligence under the Real Property Exception to the school immunity statute.

ISSUE. Pennsylvania schools enjoy immunity protection for student injuries resulting from supervisory functions. The educators are not protected for injuries resulting from the lack of care or control over property. This exclusion is called the Real Property Exception. Was the pole vaulter injured as a result of supervision or unsafe equipment?

DECISION. The use of proper matting is an essential safety element. Additionally, it is an aspect of the school's care, custody, and control of its real property. Therefore, the use and placement of landing mats fall within the immunity exception.

The defense of governmental immunity is not applicable to a school district when a student is injured by a fall from gym rings.

McCLOSKEY V. ABINGTON SCHOOL DISTRICT
515 A.2d 642
Commonwealth Court of Pennsylvania
September 29, 1986

FACTS. A 10th-grade student at Abington High School (Pennsylvania), fell from gym rings during a regularly scheduled gym class. His injury left him quadriplegic. His parents filed a lawsuit against the school district for damages. The school defended on the immunity provision of the state code which provided, in part:

> "No local agency shall be liable for any damages on account of any injury to a person or property caused by any act of the local agency or an employee thereof or any other person." (p. 643)

The trial court granted judgment to the school district. However, on appeal, the decision was reversed and a new trial was ordered because the trial court failed to consider application of the real property exception to governmental immunity.

ISSUE. When is Real Property Exception to immunity applicable?

DECISION. The defense of governmental immunity is valid when an injury occurs as the result of inadequate or incompetent supervision. However, in Pennsylvania, the immunity defense is not permitted when a public agency furnishes or has control of unsafe property or real estate.

The issues relating to the height of the gym rings, their installation and placement, or the use of protective floor mats fall under the Real Property Exception to the immunity defense. The facts regarding those issues should be determined by a jury and not by the trial court.

The Illinois Approach

In Illinois, educators are not liable for the conduct or discipline of the schools and school children, except for their wilful and wanton misconduct. This protection is based on their parental immunity. Therefore, a number of lawsuits against the schools and physical educators for physical activity injuries are based on theories other than negligence.

A trampoline is not unreasonably dangerous; its normal use in a physical education class is not a hazardous activity.

FALLON V. INDIAN TRAIL SCHOOL
500 N.E.2d 101
Appellate Court of Illinois, 2nd District
October 31, 1986

FACTS. A former student filed a lawsuit against the Indian Trail School (Illinois) for injuries she sustained when attempting a "front drop" maneuver on a trampoline during a sixth-grade physical education class. In addition to the school, she sued the two supervising physical education teachers.

She alleged, under a theory of strict liability, the school was liable for exposing her to an "ultrahazardous" activity on an abnormally dangerous instrument, and that the school was negligent in the hiring and supervision of the two physical education teachers. The court dismissed the case.

ISSUE. Persons who expose others to activities which are highly dangerous, unusual, or inappropriate to the time and place, though lawful, are "strictly liable" for any resulting harm. In this case, is a trampoline abnormally dangerous, or is its use an "ultrahazardous" activity?

DECISION. An abnormally dangerous product must be dangerous in its normal or non-defective state. And, the danger from the product must be caused from more than the mere negligence of others (in this case, the plaintiff alleged the teachers' negligence). Although there can be a negligent use of a trampoline, neither the trampoline itself nor its ordinary use are considered abnormally dangerous or "ultrahazardous" for purposes of the strict liability theory.

In *Fallon*, the plaintiff used the theory of strict liability to circumvent the immunity protecting the Illinois educators. Today, when use of trampolines in physical education classes is being discontinued by an increasing number of school districts; the *Fallon* case represents an interesting paradox. Since the court concluded that trampolines were not abnormally dangerous under a theory of strict liability, one might assume that educators in Illinois would be protected if they used trampolines in their physical education classes. However, such an assumption is wrong. As easily as the court in *Fallon* concluded that strict liability did not apply to trampoline use, Illinois courts are just as likely to impose liability for ordinary negligence in furnishing the trampoline to the physical education class in the first place. In *Ausmus v. Board of Education of the City of Chicago*, the issue centered on softball equipment.

Furnishing equipment for a physical education class is not a supervisory duty protected by immunity.

AUSMUS V. BOARD OF EDUCATION OF THE CITY OF
CHICAGO
508 N.E.2d 298
Appellate Court of Illinois, 1st District
April 16, 1987

FACTS. The mother of a third-grade student at Nathaniel Green Elementary School sued the Chicago School Board for injuries her son suffered in a softball game. He was struck in the face with a bat in a game conducted during a physical education class. Her suit alleged that the school failed to provide safe equipment for use, particularly: by permitting the use of adult size bats, failing to use safer equipment, failing to require safety helmets or face masks, failing to use a backstop or other markings to indicate batting and catching areas, and failing to provide adequate medical equipment.

The court rejected the school board's argument that it was protected by immunity from liability under Illinois law.

ISSUE. The Illinois School Code provides that educators enjoy *in loco parentis* status in all matters relating to the discipline and conduct of the schools and school children. Therefore, except for wilful and wanton misconduct, educators are immune from liability for supervisory duties. Why did the court reject the school's immunity defense?

DECISION. The court ruled the issue was furnishing unsafe equipment, not the supervision of students. It cited previous case law:

> "On the contrary, public policy considerations argue rather strongly against any interpretation which would relax a school district's obligations to insure that equipment provided for students in connection with activities of this type is *fit for the purpose.*" (p. 300)

Accordingly, the student's mother was only required to prove negligence for the failure to provide *effective* equipment. Immunity does not apply to unsafe equipment.

But, in *Braun v. Board of Education of Red Bud Community Unit School District 132*, the apparent failure to provide safer equipment did not result in liability.

In Illinois, educators are only liable for their wilful and wanton misconduct relating to the discipline and conduct of the schools.

BRAUN V. BD. OF EDUCATION OF RED BUD COMMUNITY
UNIT SCHOOL DIST. 132
502 N.E.2d 1076
Appellate Court of Illinois, 5th District
December 16, 1986

FACTS. The student-manager of a high school basketball team was injured when he blacked out and fell from an extension ladder while posting names on a scoreboard. The student was an epileptic who suffered seizures, and was warned to stay away from heights. He was working under the direction of a physical education teacher. However, the teacher said he understood the student's medical condition was under control. Neither the teacher nor the school officials were totally aware of the student's condition. The teacher directed the student to use the ladder instead of the scaffold which, allegedly, may have prevented the fall.

The student sued the school board and the teacher for their failure to provide the scaffold, but the court dismissed the case based on educational immunity.

ISSUE. In Illinois, educators are liable for:

1. wilful and wanton misconduct relating to the discipline and conduct of schools and school children; and

2. negligence for breach of duty in furnishing equipment.

Is the school's failure to provide the scaffold a supervisory decision, or a failure to furnish safe equipment?

DECISION. The scaffold was already furnished (it had been purchased and was available on the premises). However, the court ruled the teacher's failure to use it was a supervisory duty relating to the student-teacher relationship, not a breach of duty regarding property. Therefore, the student's burden of proof was to prove wilful and wanton misconduct on the part of the school or the teacher, rather than mere negligence.

The teacher had good reason to believe the student's condition was controlled. And, the school knew less than the teacher regarding the student's physical condition. Therefore, the teacher and the school lacked the requisite knowledge for their actions to be deemed wiful and wanton misconduct.

There is a subtle distinction to the decisions in the *Braun* case and the *Ausmus* case. Both cases dealt with the failure to provide proper equipment, and both examined the safety elements of the property which was provided. However, in *Braun*, the court recognized the teacher's decision to use a ladder as a supervisory function protected from liability. In *Ausmus*, the court held the teacher was liable for providing inadequate equipment. Although the distinction is apparent in the light of legal examination, those decisions and their consequences are not always obvious to the physical educator in his or her daily activities.

There is very little to distinguish a supervisory function from an equipment function. It should be assumed that decisions relating to the use of equipment are supervisory functions. However, today's physical educator must be cognizant that those functions are legally separate, as are their consequences.

Placement and maintenance of a concrete riser in a school gym is not a supervisory function protected by immunity.

PREST V. SPARTA COMMUNITY UNIT SCHOOL DISTRICT NO. 140
510 N.E.2d 595
Appellate Court of Illinois, 5th Dist.
July 1, 1987

FACTS. A student was injured when he fell against a concrete riser located in the school gym during a supervised instructional activity. His father filed a suit alleging the school was negligent in building and maintaining an unpadded concrete riser in close proximity to the gym.

The court, over the school's objections, ruled that the case had to be determined by the duty of ordinary care that a landowner owes to users on his property, not the duty of care owed by educators to their students.

ISSUE. The Illinois School Code had a provision that educators, in the discipline and conduct of the schools stood in the same relation as parents to the students (*in loco parentis*). The effect of the parental immunity was that educators were immune from liability for injury resulting from negligent conduct. However, they were liable for wilful and wanton misconduct.

Why didn't the court apply the Illinois School Code?

DECISION. The court distinguished the school code from the allegations in this case. It noted that parental immunity extended only to supervisory conduct, not the maintenance of property, which was a *separate function*. The court equated the separate function to cases involving defective personal property. For example, furnishing a defective football helmet is not considered a supervisory activity. Thus, a school may be liable for its failure to exercise ordinary care in the furnishing of helmet, yet it enjoys parental immunity for its negligent supervision of football practice.

There was strong dissent to this opinion from one Justice who stated that the statute encompassed all activities, and, in this instance, it was impossible to separate supervision from the physical condition of the building.

WILFUL AND WANTON MISCONDUCT

Wilful and wanton misconduct impacts on the traditional immunity protection afforded physical educators. Again, wilful and wanton misconduct is a very severe form of negligence, which is usually evidenced by an intentional disregard for the safety of others. (Negligence does not require any intentional conduct on the part of the wrongdoer.)

When an educator has knowledge of an unreasonable risk of danger to his students and has knowledge that other students have previously suffered injuries as a result of that risk, or a similar risk, he is liable. When, in the face of that knowledge, he makes no effort to adequately warn of or correct the danger, the educator can be liable for wilful and wanton misconduct. There are other factors unique to physical education which may be considered wilful and wanton misconduct. First, the physical educator who teaches minor school children is held to a higher degree of care, since it is presumed the educator is sensitive to the immaturity of the pupils. Second, since the physical education activities may have a higher degree of risk than classroom activities, it is presumed that the physical educator will take the requisite care in the supervision of those student activities.

Wilful and wanton misconduct is intentional behavior which exhibits reckless disregard for the safety of others.

TIJERINA V. EVANS
501 N.E.2d 995
Appellate Court of Illinois, 2nd District
December 10, 1986

FACTS. A student at Glenbard North High School (Illinois) was injured in a whiffle ball game conducted during a physical education class. The defendant, a physical education teacher, was supervising the class at the time of the injury. The game was held in the school gymnasium. The student was injured when he ran into the first row of bleachers which had been pulled out and locked in place.

He filed a lawsuit against the teacher and the School District alleging wilful and wanton misconduct. The case was dismissed when the court ruled the student failed to allege the necessary elements for a claim based on wilful and wanton misconduct.

ISSUE. What are the elements of wilful and wanton misconduct?

DECISION. Wilful and wanton misconduct requires an intentional act which is committed in reckless disregard for the safety of others. It is easily distinguishable from mere negligence which is not based on intentional acts.

The student's complaint failed to specify how the game of whiffle ball within the confines of the gym was more dangerous than other activities conducted in the gym, and how the exposed first row of the bleachers created a danger sufficient to justify wilful and wanton misconduct. While the student, arguably, had alleged the necessary elements for a negligence suit, he failed to plead a case which met the requirements of wilful and wanton misconduct. Without an allegation of intentional behavior on the part of the defendant, the court could not establish if there was a reckless disregard for the student's safety.

The major consequences of wilful and wanton misconduct are threefold. Neither a school, nor its staff and faculty are protected by statutory or common law immunity for wilful and wanton misconduct. School board members, administrators, and staff members can be held personally liable for the injuries suffered by a student resulting from wilful and wanton misconduct. Finally, wilful and wanton misconduct can result in the award of punitive damages against the educator and the school district. Those are damages awarded to the injured party in addition to, or in excess of, the actual or compensatory damages for the injury.[2]

Inadequate supervision of a school locker room is not wilful and wanton misconduct.

HOLSAPPLE V. CASEY COMMUNITY UNIT SCHOOL DISTRICT
C-1
510 N.E.2d 499
Appellate Court of Illinois, 4th Dist.
June 24, 1987

FACTS. The plaintiff, a student, became involved in an altercation with another student in the school locker room during a school athletic event. Part of of the plaintiff's small finger was amputated when the other student slammed a door on his hand. The plaintiff sued the school for its wanton and wilful misconduct by failing to supervise the locker room, and for the school's failure to install a door with a spring loaded or pneumatic device to retard its closing. The court denied the claim.

ISSUE. In Illinois, a plaintiff must prove wilful and wanton misconduct by educators in the discipline and conduct of schools before the law will impose liability. Wilful and wanton misconduct is either conduct intended to harm, or the failure to exercise ordinary care to prevent injury from a known impending danger. Does the failure to supervise student activities constitute such conduct?

DECISION. The failure to adequately supervise the locker room was not wilful and wanton misconduct. The court determined that the plaintiff had to prove the school was aware of a high probability of serious harm before it would impose such a severe degree of liability. The plaintiff failed to meet that burden.

The court also rejected plaintiff's contention that the school failed to exercise ordinary care in maintaining the door. Plaintiff did not prove the door was inherently dangerous. It was neither a swinging or revolving door, nor did it contain glass. Therefore, the door operated as it was designed, and the school was under no obligation to install a different door.

The significance of the *Tijerina* and *Holsapple* decisions is not that plaintiffs will have a difficult time establishing wilful and wanton misconduct, rather that plaintiffs are alleging more varied forms of wilful and wanton misconduct.

ADDITIONAL ISSUES

The following two cases provide additional reference for physical educators. Since the emphasis of this chapter has been the increased duty of care owed by physical educators, it should be assumed that job qualifications will be heavily scrutinized. In *Zink v. Board of Education of Chrisman*, the court examined whether state certification was qualification for a specific teaching position in physical education.

State certification to teach physical education is not sufficient qualification for a specific physical education position.

ZINK V. BOARD OF EDUCATION OF CHRISMAN
497 N.E.2d 835
Appellate Court of Illinois
September 3, 1986

FACTS. A home economics teacher at the Chrisman Community School (Illinois) received her teaching certificate in 1961. She was certified, in addition to other subjects, for physical education. In the spring of 1983, she was notified that her home economics position was being reduced to part-time due to a reduction in force policy. She petitioned the school board to "bump" the full-time tenured physical education teacher who lacked her seniority.

When the school board denied her petition, she filed a lawsuit seeking the full-time physical education position per Illinois Tenure law. The court ruled she was *not* qualified for the specific position.

ISSUE. Under Illinois law, the home economics teacher held seniority over the full-time physical education teacher. If she was qualified for the position, the school board would be required to "bump" the present full-time physical education teacher, and award her the position. Was her 1961 certification sufficient qualification for the position?

DECISION. Although the 1961 certification allowed her to teach physical education, the teacher had neither teaching experience nor any recent course work in physical education. On that basis, being legally qualified to teach physical education was distinguished from the legal qualifications for a specific position in physical education.

A local school board is granted some discretion in determining reasonable requirements for the job. As an example, male locker room supervision was one of the duties for which the full-time physical education teacher was responsible, and for which the home economics teacher was not qualified.

Can students create unreasonable risks of danger for their teachers? In *Melder v. State Farm Fire and Casualty Company*, the court looked at the knowledge, appreciation, and voluntary encounter of a risk to determine if a student was liable for the injuries to a teacher aide.

A teacher aide who is struck by a ball while observing a physical education class has not been exposed to an unreasonable risk.

MELDER V. STATE FARM FIRE & CASUALTY COMPANY
498 So.2d 1095
Court of Appeal of Louisiana, 3rd Circuit
December 10, 1986

FACTS. A high school teacher aide was unintentionally struck by a ball thrown by a student during a supervised physical education class. The participating students were playing a game similar to "dodge ball." The aide was observing the game from a doorway in the gymnasium.

The aide sued the parents of the student who had thrown the ball, but the court ruled that the young man was not negligent.

ISSUE. Does the student have a duty to protect a teacher's aide from accidentally being struck by the ball?

DECISION. The court said the aide was a spectator at a sports activity. Therefore, the only duty the student owed her was to protect her from an unreasonable risk of harm. Since the aide had observed the students playing this game on previous occasions, she had knowledge of the risk, and the opportunity to avoid the potential danger. Therefore, the risk of harm was not considered unreasonable.

REFERENCES

Adams, S., M. Adrian, and M.A. Bayless. 1987. *Catastrophic Injuries in Sports: Avoidance Strategies.* 2nd ed. 3-13, 259- 264. Indianapolis, IN: Benchmark Press, Inc.

Alexander, K. and M.D. Alexander. 1984. *The Law of Schools, Students, and Teachers.* Nutshell Series: 147-161, 204-235. St. Paul, MN: West Publishing Co.

Peterson, L., R. Rossmiller, and M. Volz. 1978. *The Law and Public School Operation.* 2nd ed., 1-32, 251-265. New York, NY: Harper and Row, Publishers, Inc.

[1] *In loco parentis* status, or parental immunity, does not protect the educator for his or her wilful and wanton misbehavior, or intentional misbehavior. The immunity applies only to negligent conduct.

[2] Punitive damages reflect society's civil punishment for serious misconduct or malicious misconduct. Since many jurisdictions do not require a ratio or proportion of actual or compensatory damages to punitive damages, it is possible to have an actual damage that is insignificant and a punitive damage that is very large.

Chapter 4

Athletic Associations

INTRODUCTION

The athletic association was formed because of the need to standardize playing rules for competitive sports; it was the logical result of the efforts of athletic administrators to insure fair play and equal competition in sports. Since athletic associations fulfilled a recognized need through voluntary participation, there were few problems in attracting an interested membership. However, as the associations grew in members and stature, they also began to assume other roles as well, specifically, regulatory administration.[1]

The National Basketball Association's rule governing franchise relocation is valid.

NATIONAL BASKETBALL ASSOCIATION V. SDC BASKETBALL CLUB
815 F.2d 562
United States Court of Appeals, 9th Circuit
April 21, 1987

FACTS. The San Diego Clippers, a member of the National Basketball Association (NBA), moved their franchise to Los Angeles without formal approval of the NBA. The NBA had a rule governing franchise relocation. However, the Clippers move came on the heels of a federal court ruling that allowed the relocation of the National Football League's (NFL) Raiders to Los Angeles. The NFL was found to have violated restraint of trade under antitrust laws by attempting to deny that franchise relocation.

The NBA filed a suit against the Clippers, which was dismissed by the trial court on the basis of the Raiders' ruling. However, on appeal, the United States Court of Appeals reversed the trial court. It ruled the Raiders' decision was valid only for the Raiders' move and did not constitute an absolute rule of law regarding franchise relocation rules for professional sports leagues.

ISSUE. Are there legal limitations in professional sports when a professional team wants to relocate to another city?

DECISION. While a sports league would be wise to implement objective procedures for franchise relocation evaluation, such procedures are not necessary conditions to the legality of franchise relocation rules. However, the NBA asserted that it used a variety of criteria in evaluating franchise movements, and that its market was substantially different from the NFL.

The Raiders' case examined the professional football market, the history and purpose of the NFL's Franchise Movement Rule, and its application to antitrust provisions. The case did not set forth an absolute rule of law regarding franchise movement in professional sports.

It is important to distinguish assumed duties from delegated duties. In many instances, the rule-making authority of voluntary associations was implicitly delegated by their members. As the social role of competitive sports grew through the years, its regulation was actively separated from judicial or legislative controls. In response, the athletic associations expanded their roles to meet the ever-increasing problems created by the public's growing interest in competitive athletics.

The regulatory freedom enjoyed by voluntary associations has few limitations. Since its source of power is derived from the legitimate, voluntary participation of the membership, the courts are very reluctant to interfere in the rule-making or rule-enforcement of an association. A rule or its application must be unreasonable and arbitrary, or must violate a protected constitutional right before the courts will intervene.[2] Recently, one of the most important, and challenged, regulatory functions has been determining who may participate—*eligibility*.

HIGH SCHOOL ASSOCIATIONS

One of the primary distinctions between state high school athletic associations and collegiate or professional associations is that the high school athletic participation, or its resulting benefit, is not a constitutionally-protected right. Many actions challenging the eligibility rules of athletic associations have focused on high school athletic participation as part of the compulsory education process; the large majority of the actions have failed. In *Mississippi High School Activities Association, Inc. v. Farris*, the court ruled there was not a constitutional right to play high school baseball.

High school baseball players may not assert the same rights granted to their school as a member of a high school athletic association.

MISSISSIPPI HIGH SCHOOL ACTIVITIES ASSOCIATION, INC.
V. FARRIS
501 So.2d 393
Supreme Court of Mississippi
January 14, 1987

FACTS. The Hattiesburg High School (Mississippi) baseball team was playing a game in a tournament sponsored by the Mississippi High School Activities Association (MHSAA). The Hattiesburg coach was ejected from the game. When he refused to leave the field, the umpire declared the game a forfeit in favor of the other team. The MHSAA, without hearing, placed Hattiesburg on probation and eliminated them from the tournament.

The team members filed a lawsuit asking the court that they be permitted to play in the tournament. They argued that their elimination from the tournament meant they could not display their baseball skills for college scholarship purposes. The case went to the Mississippi Supreme Court which denied the request since there was not a constitutional right to play baseball.

ISSUE. Do the team members have any right to assert a claim against the MHSAA? Is the expectation of a college baseball scholarship a constitutionally-protected right?

DECISION. The Court ruled the team members were not third party beneficiaries to the membership agreement of their high school and the MHSAA. The MHSAA membership directly benefitted the high school, and only incidentally benefitted the team members.

Hattiesburg High School was not prevented from enforcing its own rights with the MHSAA. Therefore, the team members did not have the right to assert those rights on behalf of the high school.

The expectation of a college athletic scholarship is not a legitimate property right protected by constitutional safeguards, nor is the right to play baseball enforceable under the same constitutional requirements that guarantee a right to a public education.

Because of its close involvement with public education, a state high school athletic association is considered to directly represent the state. That involvement serves as the requisite judicial standing (called "state action") for filing constitutional claims against associations.

The eligibility regulations of high school athletic associations have two purposes: to insure equal competition among the participants, and to prevent recruiting of high school athletes. Transfer eligibility and age eligibility are two of the most challenged rules by high school athletes and their families. However, the courts have consistently ruled that regulations which prevent unfair competition, redshirting, and high school recruiting are legitimate objectives.

Many high school athletic associations have procedures that permit waivers when an association regulation would create an undue and severe hardship. It is the failure of many athletic associations to uniformly or equitably grant waivers that has led to the growing number of lawsuits testing eligibility issues. In *Zuments v. Colorado High School Activities Association*, the association waiver policy was upheld by the court because it was applied uniformly; in *Staten v. Couch*, a school district's waiver policy was disallowed by the court because it lacked guidelines and review procedures.

A high school activities association waiver policy for the outside competition rule does not violate equal protection of the laws.

ZUMENTS V. COLORADO HIGH SCHOOL
ACTIVITIES ASSOCIATION
737 P.2d 1113
Colorado Court of Appeals, Div. II
April 2, 1987

FACTS. Some Colorado High School student-athletes filed suit against the Colorado High School Activities Association (CHSAA) for its failure to waive the Association's "outside competition" rule. Specifically, that rule provides:

> "Players certified to participate as members of any high school sport may not compete on any other team, nor in any non-school activity or event in that sport during that sports season." (p. 1114)

The students claimed that CHSAA's enforcement of the rule in their case was unconstitutional because the Association had granted waivers for other athletes who competed in international competition or for teams recognized by the U.S. Olympic Committee, or with approval of the appropriate high school principal.

ISSUE. Is the strict application of outside competition rule arbitrary, capricious, and haphazard, so it violates the student-athletes constitutional rights?

DECISION. The court ruled there was not a constitutionally-protected right to participate in athletics, so the rule could not violate due process rights, nor did the rule impinge on any rights of free association since its purpose was only to set the terms and conditions for participation in athletics.

The court denied the students claim, however, because the waiver policy was uniformly applied to all athletes for the approved meets. There were no records of one student being granted a waiver to a meet, while another student was denied a waiver to the same meet. Waivers were granted for all approved meets, and were not granted for non-approved meets. In summary, the court found no basis to substantiate the finding that the waiver provision was arbitrary, capricious, or haphazard.

A county school board's transfer eligibility rule violates constitutional due process.

STATEN V. COUCH
507 So.2d 702
District Court of Appeal of Florida, 1st Dist.
May 14, 1987

FACTS. The plaintiff attended Rickards High School (Florida) for two years during which time he played interscholastic basketball. He requested a transfer to Godby High School which was located in another school zone within Leon County. Godby offered the only ROTC program in the county. The Leon County School Board approved the academic transfer, but the principal of Rickards High School refused to sign a waiver to permit the plaintiff to participate in any co-curricular activities at Godby.

The Leon County School Board had a regulation which prohibited transfer students from other school zones within the county from participating in co-curricular activities unless he or she had a waiver from the principal of the school the student was leaving. Conceivably, a student's extracurricular participation could be denied the four years the student was at the non-zoned school.

The Leon County School Board amended the rule so he could participate in co-curricular activities after completion of one year at Godby High School.

The student sued the school board. The court ruled that the regulation violated constitutional due process.

ISSUE. The Rickards' principal refused to sign a waiver because: other principals had refused to sign waivers for him; the student was reassigned for academic, not athletic, reasons; and, Rickards High School had a decreasing school population which caused professional disadvantages for the school and the principal.

DECISION. The court noted that the school board's own witnesses conceded there was no improper motive for the student's requested transfer to Godby High School. It was evident from the school board's hearing of the student's appeal that there were no guidelines for transfer eligibility, nor were there any substantive procedures permitting an appeal when a waiver was denied.

The regulation violated due process because it lacked standards, express or otherwise, by which the principal's exercise of discretion could be understood by students or parents; or, applied in a manner allowing proper grievance or review proceedings.

Transfer Eligibility

A transfer eligibility rule usually specifies that a student who transfers from one high school to another is not eligible for athletic competition at the new school for one semester or more, if the student's move was for athletic reasons or if the family residence of the athlete was not changed.

The basis for a student's school transfer usually includes a change of residence by the student and his parents, or guardians, before the student will be eligible for competition at the new school. However, a legitimate academic purpose for the transfer does not serve as a basis for a waiver of the rule by an association, as was demonstrated in *Berschback v. Grosse Pointe Public School District.*

The Michigan High School Athletic Association's transfer eligibility rule does not violate constitutional guarantees.

BERSCHBACK V. GROSSE POINTE PUBLIC SCHOOL DISTRICT
397 N.W.2d 234
Court of Appeals of Michigan
August 18, 1986

FACTS. A student transferred from her private high school to the public high school located within her school district. When she transferred, she learned that she was ineligible for athletic competition for one semester at the public high school. Another student transferred from a private high school to the public high school within his school district, and found that he was ineligible for athletic competition for one semester, thus denying him the opportunity to play football. Both students transferred for legitimate educational purposes. The students were declared ineligible under the Mighigan High School Athletic Association's (MHSAA) Transfer Eligibility Rule.

The students lawsuits, challenging the Transfer Eligibility Rule on constitutional grounds, were dismissed.

ISSUE. The MHSAA Transfer Eligibility Rule states that a student who transfers from one high school to another is ineligible to participate in interscholastic athletics for one semester at the school where he or she transfers.

The MHSAA has a number of exceptions to the rule; additionally, the association has the authority to waive the rule if it fails to accomplish the purpose for which it is intended. If the transfers were for legitimate educational purposes, should the rule be waived?

DECISION. The purpose of the Transfer Eligibility Rule was to prevent recruiting at the high school level. Because the rule has a legitimate objective and the MHSAA has a waiver policy, the regulation does not violate Equal Protection of the Laws.

Participation in athletics is not a property or liberty right protected by the Constitution. It is not recognized as a component of compulsory classroom attendance and education, nor are athletics mandated as courses of instruction. Participation is permissive. Thus, while application of the Transfer Eligibility Rule may sometimes be "heavy-handed," it is not a denial of constitutionally-protected rights.

The high school athletic association enjoys dual legal protection. It is recognized by the courts as the state regulatory agency for interscholastic athletics; therefore, most association rules have a judicially legitimate purpose. The association is also a voluntary organization, which means that the rights and privileges its members share are granted only through membership. If a school does not wish to be a member and abide by the association rules, the school is free to quit.[3]

Illinois students who transfer from private high schools to public high schools will be granted immediate athletic eligibility.

GRIFFIN HIGH SCHOOL V. ILLINOIS HIGH SCHOOL
ASSOCIATION
822 F.2d 671
United States Court of Appeals, 7th Circuit
June 10, 1987

FACTS. Griffin High School, a private religious high school member of the Illinois High School Association (IHSA), filed suit against that association because it adopted a rule which granted immediate athletic eligibility to students who transferred from private schools to public schools.

The IHSA supervised and regulated the interscholastic activities of its members. Prior to adoption of the new rule, students who transferred from one member school to another member school were ineligible for athletic participation for one year, unless the student's parents had actually changed their residence to the new school district. The court rejected the argument that the new rule violated Griffin High School's constitutional rights.

ISSUE. Griffin High School alleged the new IHSA transfer rule was discriminatory because it interfered with the free exercise of religion and the rights of parents to direct the education of their children.

DECISION. The plaintiff did not show how the rule affected the school's religious tenets, or caused students to perform acts which were contradictory to their fundamental religious beliefs. The contention that the rule interfered with parents ability to direct the education of their children was too speculative.

The rule was based on the IHSA's dissatisfaction with the inequitable competition between public and private schools. Specifically, the private schools could select students from an unlimited geographical area, provided scholarships and tuition waivers as incentives, and could choose and control their enrollment. These functions were not available to public schools. Those differences were considered inequities by the IHSA. The intent of the new rule was to remedy the inequities in furtherance of a legitimate purpose, that is, to prevent the recruitment of high school athletes.

The court noted that the plaintiff never attended any of the meetings of the legislative body, failed to submit proposals or amendments, and otherwise ignored the decision-making process, while the rule was under consideration.

The most requested legal remedy in a case challenging an association transfer eligibility rule is an injunction. If an athlete is facing imminent ineligibility, he or she may petition for an injunction permitting participation until the full merits of the case can be heard. In *University Interscholastic League v. Jones*, the delay in appeal process rendered the athletic association's objection to an injunction meaningless since the competitive season in question was completed when the case came to court.

An athletic association's appeal of a student-athlete's successful lawsuit after completion of the athletic season is moot.

UNIVERSITY INTERSCHOLASTIC LEAGUE V. JONES
715 S.W.2d 759
Court of Appeals of Texas
July 23, 1986

FACTS. A Texas high school football player moved with his family from McArthur High School to the Highland Park High School district prior to the 1985 football season. The Texas University Interscholastic League (UIL), which regulates interscholastic athletics in Texas, ruled the family move was only for athletic purposes and declared the student ineligible to play football his senior year at Highland Park High School.

The player was ineligible under the following UIL rule:

> "A student who changes schools for athletic purposes is not eligible to compete in varsity league athletic contests at the school to which he moves for at least one calendar year." (p. 760)

The student and his family petitioned the court for a permanent injunction to allow him to play and to prevent the UIL from imposing sanctions against Highland Park High School for permitting his participation. The injunction was granted, and the UIL appealed to the Texas Court of Appeals. However, since the appeal came after the 1985 football season was completed, the appeal was dismissed.

ISSUE. Should the Texas Court of Appeals consider the propriety of the UIL's appeal and render a decision regarding the eligibility rule for future cases?

DECISION. The court stated that its function was not to render decisions or opinions on past disputes.

> "The law is well settled in this state that courts are created not for the purposes of deciding abstract or academic questions of law or render advisory opinions, but solely for the judicial determination of presently existing disputes between the parties in which an effective judgment can be rendered." (p. 761)

Age Eligibility

The age eligibility rules usually render any student, who attains his or her 19th birthday before September 1st, ineligible for athletics during the ensuing school year.

Age eligibility is an arbitrary concept. However, there are very good reasons for insuring equal competition between athletes of similar maturity. Since date selection is random, caution must be taken by the association to insure its fair and equitable application.

An athletic association's unwritten policy of not granting waivers is unlawful since it is directly contrary to its own written rules.

TIFFANY V. ARIZONA INTERSCHOLASTIC ASSOCIATION
726 P.2d 231
Court of Appeals of Arizona
June 12, 1986

FACTS. The Arizona Interscholastic Association's (AIA) age classification rule prohibited high school athletes from participating in athletics during the school year if their 19th birthday was before September 1st of that school year. The plaintiff, an athlete entering his senior year of high school, had been held back in school during kindergarten and first grade due to a learning disability. His 19th birthday occurred on August 5th prior to his senior year. The AIA refused to waive the age rule upon his eligibility request.

The plaintiff was granted an injunction allowing him to compete. The AIA's appeal to the Arizona Court of Appeals was dismissed when that court found the AIA had acted in an unreasonable, capricious, and arbitrary manner in refusing the student's waiver request.

ISSUE. The Arizona Interscholastic Association had a discretion rule which stated:

> "The Executive Board in individual cases may, at its discretion and upon such terms and conditions as it may impose, waive or modify any eligibility rule when in its opinion there are circumstances beyond the control of the student or parent whereby enforcement of the rule would work an undue hardship on the student. . ." (p. 232)

DECISION. The Executive Board of the AIA had an unwritten policy of never permitting waivers to the 19 year age rule. Therefore, by denying the student's waiver petition, the AIA acted unlawfully because the no exception policy was contrary to their written rule.

The student also argued that he had a constitutional right to participate in high school athletics. Traditionally, the courts have refused to recognize such participation as constitutionally-protected. The Arizona Court of Appeals noted, however, there might be circumstances when an athlete could establish a right to due process protection stemming from a suspension or exclusion from high school athletics.

It should be noted that age classification rules serve a specific purpose. Therefore, a claim alleging a severe hardship must be able to show how application of the rule fails to serve a legitimate interest, as in *Nichols v. Farmington Public Schools.*

The athletic association age classification rule has a legitimate objective.

NICHOLS V. FARMINGTON PUBLIC SCHOOLS
389 N.W.2d 480
Court of Appeals of Michigan
April 9, 1986

FACTS. Prior to his high school senior year, the plaintiff was declared ineligible to compete in varsity basketball because his 19th birthday occurred prior to September 1st of the school year. The Michigan High School Athletic Association (MHSAA) had an age classification rule which denied athletic eligibility to anyone whose 19th birthday occurs before September 1st of the school year.

The plaintiff, a handicapped youngster who suffered a severe hearing disorder, was "mainstreamed" from special education classes to regular elementary classes in 1976. He failed to meet the MHSAA age requirement because he was placed in a grade one year below his age level at the time of that transfer. His claim that the age classification rule violated his constitutional right of due process was dismissed.

ISSUE. Should the MHSAA waive its age classification rule in this case since the elementary grade placement was made to accommodate a handicapped child?

DECISION. The court ruled that due process rights were not violated because the student's parents never requested a hearing. Further, they did not object to the boy's placement in regular elementary classes in 1976.

The age classification rule is recognized in interscholastic athletics throughout the United States. It is intended to promote equality in competition, and discourage the concept of red-shirting.

NATIONAL COLLEGIATE ATHLETIC ASSOCIATION

The National Collegiate Athletic Association, as its high school counterparts, is a voluntary association. Therefore, while its members enjoy privileges of membership, they also are bound by the rules of the organization. There is a fallacy to the voluntary organization concept: the NCAA's members include all the major universities who participate in football or basketball at the Division One level. A major university football power who doesn't like an NCAA rule can discontinue its membership in the organization; but, with whom will the school compete if it wishes to continue its football tradition?

This should not serve as a caustic reflection on the power of the NCAA. However, the courts generally value the voluntary association. Justifiably, the courts will protect the rights of members to regulate themselves, or to delegate that authority to their voluntary association. Therefore, to *successfully* challenge the rules of the NCAA, a member must be prepared to challenge the inherent purpose of the organization itself.

There are three very distinct and important differences between the NCAA and high school athletic organizations. First, the NCAA governs from a national organization; high school athletic associations serve within state borders. Second, eligibility for collegiate athletics, and its implicit benefits, may have a profound property interest protected by the constitution. Again, high school athletic participation is not so protected. Third, the NCAA is recognized as the representative for all its members in matters dealing with athletic regulation; high school associations must contend with the legitimate authority of their local school boards, as well as the state department of education. In *Kneeland v. National Collegiate Athletic Association*, the court was asked to determine whether the NCAA could legally represent its members' interests to rights of privacy.

Southern Methodist University and Rice University cannot intervene in a lawsuit regarding the disclosure of NCAA investigations.

KNEELAND V. NATIONAL COLLEGIATE ATHLETIC
ASSOCIATION
806 F.2d 1285
United States Court of Appeals, 5th Circuit
January 7, 1987

The Federal Rules of Civil Procedure (Fed. R. Civ. P. 24[a]) permits a party to "intervene" in a lawsuit when the subject of the lawsuit relates to an interest of that party. It provides, in part:

"Upon timely application anyone shall be permitted to intervene in an action: . . . or (2) when the applicant claims an interest relating to the property or transaction which is the subject of the action and he is so situated that the disposition of the action may as a practical matter impair or impede his ability to protect that interest, unless the applicant's interest is adequately represented by existing parties."

FACTS. The plaintiffs filed a suit to compel the NCAA to turn over records of its investigation of the Southern Methodist University (SMU) football program since 1980. The suit was later expanded to include investigations of all members of the Southwest Conference. The requests of Rice University and Southern Methodist University, both members of the NCAA and the Southwest Conference, to intervene in the case were denied by the court.

ISSUE. Do SMU and Rice have the right to assert their rights to privacy, academic freedom, freedom of association, and other privileges as defenses to disclosure of the investigation documents though they are not a party to the lawsuit?

DECISION. The universities are voluntary members of the NCAA. And, the common objective of SMU, Rice, and the NCAA is to prevent disclosure of the investigation documents. Thus, the NCAA and the Southwest Conference have the legal standing to raise any defenses on behalf of their members.

Accordingly, SMU and Rice do not have the right to intervene as parties in the suit, per Rule 24(a) of the Rules of Federal Civil Procedure.

Professional Affiliation

A student-athlete forfeits his or her collegiate eligibility when the athlete signs a professional contract. The primary philosophy of the NCAA is predicated on preserving the amateur status of collegiate athletics. Regardless of the intentions of the athlete, the NCAA protects the spirit and the letter of that prohibition.

The NCAA rule prohibiting professional participation does not violate constitutional guarantees.

KARMANOS V. BAKER
816 F.2d 258
United States Court of Appeals, 6th Circuit
April 20, 1987

FACTS. A hockey player, upon completion of his Canadian high school education, played ice hockey in the Canadian Major Junior A Hockey League. However, he played with a contract that specified that he would not be paid any compensation, and that he would be responsible for his own expenses.

The NCAA prohibits an individual from participating on a professional team. And, the Canadian league had previously been ruled to be a professional league by the NCAA. When he enrolled at the University of Michigan, the plaintiff was declared ineligible to play intercollegiate hockey.

The court dismissed his claim that the NCAA rule violated his constitutional right of freedom of association with professional hockey players.

ISSUE. Is there a constitutionally-protected right to play hockey?

DECISION. There is not a constitutional right to play intercollegiate hockey. In regard to the specific claims, the hockey player was not barred from "associating" with professional hockey players, he was barred from playing college hockey.

Constitutional Claims

When an eligibility rule of the NCAA is questionned on the constitutional grounds of equal protection or due process, it is up to the athlete to prove that a "state action" is involved. Does the action of the NCAA have the indirect effect of a governmental action? There have been cases that held that NCAA actions were the equivalent of state actions because many of the members were state-funded institutions, or that most of the members received federal funding. Overall, the NCAA has been subject to claims based on state action due to its pervasive influence in collegiate sports.

NCAA's transfer rule and five-year eligibility rule do not violate constitutional rights of due process or access to the courts.

GRAHAM V. NATIONAL COLLEGIATE ATHLETIC
ASSOCIATION
804 F.2d 953
United States Court of Appeals, 6th Circuit
November 6, 1986

FACTS. The plaintiff was awarded a football scholarship at the University of Louisville for the 1983 season. However, prior to the season, he withdrew from school, and the University cancelled his scholarship. He chose to complete, at his own expense, the fall semester at Louisville. He then successfully sued to have his scholarship reinstated. The university paid for his tuition, board, and fees, but denied his readmittance to the football team because of the lawsuit.

In the fall 1984, he transferred to Western Kentucky but was declared ineligible for one year pursuant to the NCAA transfer eligibility rule. Additionally, at the time of his transfer, he was in his fifth and final year of eligibility under the NCAA five-year eligibility rule.

His lawsuit against the NCAA for violation of his constitutional right was dismissed.

ISSUE. Did the NCAA violate the player's constitutional rights when he was denied eligibility for the transfer to Western Kentucky, and because the one year period of ineligibility would also toll the five-year eligibility rule?

DECISION. Since the regulation of intercollegiate athletics is *not* a state or governmental function, and since the player did not allege that the University of Louisville, as a state-supported institution, controlled or directed the application of the transfer and five-year rules, he had no basis for a constitutional claim.

His argument failed, essentially because Western Kentucky did not permit him to play football, not the University of Louisville.

STATE ATHLETIC COMMISSIONS

The authority of state athletic commissions is vested directly by the state government for the regulation of specific sports. The regulation process generally involves the licensing of participants and promoters; the sports usually included are those identified with legalized gambling or winner's purses (horse racing, boxing, and auto racing). Because the commissions are agencies of the state, their actions must comply with constitutional standards, as in *Levinson v. Washington Horse Racing Commission* and *Tattrie v. Commonwealth, Pennsylvania State Athletic Commission.*

A racing commission rule which disqualified a wife from entering horses in races because her husband had a prior felony conviction is a denial of the constitutional right to marry.

LEVINSON V. WASHINGTON HORSE RACING COMMISSION
740 P.2d 898
Court of Appeals of Washington
August 10, 1987

FACTS. The plaintiff was granted an owner's license for race horses. She listed herself as single, and used her personal funds to purchase horses. However, she was married to a man who had a previous felony drug conviction.

When it was discovered the plaintiff was married to a convicted felon, the Washington Horse Racing Commission revoked her license. Since her husband, as a convicted felon, would not have been allowed on race track property under rules of the Commission, the plaintiff also was disqualified by another rule which prohibited a spouse from entering horses in races if the other spouse was disqualified.

The plaintiff filed a lawsuit against the Commission. The Washington Court of Appeals ruled that the regulations of the Horse Racing Commission infringed on her constitutional right to marry.

ISSUE. Regulations affecting basic constitutional rights must have a rational relationship to a state interest. Is the integrity of horse racing an important state interest?

DECISION. The court rejected the Commission's argument because the rule banning the husband from race tracks (thus disqualifying the wife from entering race horses) was too broad. First of all, it directly conflicted with Washington's criminal rehabilitation act which stated that a person could not be denied licensing for any trade or business solely due to a prior felony conviction.

Second, the evidence was clear that the wife was not attempting to evade the rules or regulations of the Commission simply because she did not portray herself as married. In fact, she was unaware of her husband's previous conviction, and he had nothing to do with the ownership or maintenance of the horses. Lacking any evidence that her ownership was a sham intended to evade Commission regulations, the disqualification rules were a denial of her right to marry.

Finally, the court added that the revocation of her license was done without regard to procedural due process rights since she did not have actual notice that the board considered her actions to be misrepresentations.

The Pennsylvania State Athletic Commission is required to set a schedule of fees for physicians and referees.

TATTRIE V. COMMONWEALTH, PENNSYLVANIA STATE
ATHLETIC COMMISSION
521 A.2d 970
Commonwealth Court of Pennsylvania
February 27, 1987

FACTS. A Pennsylvania wrestling promoter conducted a wrestling match in compliance with the Pennsylvania State Athletic Commission (PSAC) rules which required a physician, a referee, and a deputy commissioner from the PSAC be in attendance. During the intermission, the promoter was informed by the deputy commissioner that the physician's fee would be $150.00, and the referee's fee would be $100.00. The promoter refused to pay those amounts, stating the fees were unreasonable and in excess of past practice.

His PSAC license was suspended when he proceeded to promote a subsequent wrestling match with a physician and referee of his own choice, without PSAC approval. The court reinstated the promoter's license over the objection of the Commission.

ISSUE. The Pennsylvania Athletic Code provides, in part:

> " . . . the Commission (PSAC) shall establish by rule or regulation a schedule of fees to be paid such physicians for their services." (p. 974)

Did the promoter violate PSAC rules?

DECISION. The Court acknowledged PSAC jurisdiction over wrestling matches, its right to assign officials and physicians for matches, and its authority to set the fees for physicians and referees.

The PSAC stated there was not a schedule of fees because time and travel were variable costs. The court agreed, but stated that a schedule could include those contingencies. Without a set fee schedule, the potential for abuse was self-evident.

The PSAC was authorized to set reasonable and equitable fees. But, the court ruled that setting referee fees at the intermission of a match was unreasonable. The regulation of referee fees should provide fair notice so a party knows precisely what is required to conform with PSAC regulations.

126

REFERENCES

Appenzeller, H. 1975. *Athletics and the Law*. 108-112 Charlottesville, VA: The Michie Company.

Berry, R. and G. Wong. 1986. *Law and Business of the Sports Industries*. Vol II: 1-94. Dover, MA: Auburn House Publishing Company.

Grieve, A. 1969. *The Legal Aspects of Athletics*. 132-143. New York, NY: A.S. Barnes and Company.

Indiana High School Athletic Association, 1985/1986, 1986/1987. *By-Laws and Articles of Incorporation*.

Schubert, G., R.K. Smith, and J.C. Trentadue. 1986. *Sports Law*. 1-39. St. Paul, MN: West Publishing Co.

State High School Athletic Associations: When Will a Court Interfere. 1971. 36 Mo. L. Rev. 400, 402-406.

[1] "As time went on it became increasingly evident that the IHSAA should assume the initiative for a well-balanced athletic program to meet the needs of *all* (emphasis added) schools and all students desiring to participate in athletics." Part VI, *By-Laws and Articles of Incorporation*, Indiana High School Athletic Association 1985/1986, p. 72.

[2] "Internal affairs, rules, and by-laws of a voluntary association should not be subject to judicial interference unless their enforcement would be arbitrary, capricious, or an abuse of discretion; where the rules are reasonable and in keeping with public policy, there will be no judicial interference." *Hebert v. Ventetuolo*, 480 A.2d 403 (1984).

[3] Membership in the state high school athletic association was a "practical necessity" according the Washington Supreme Court in *Darrin v. Gould*, 540 P.2d 882 (Wash. 1975). The court issued that opinion in a sex discrimination case filed by two female students. The court noted that most high schools in the state belonged to the Washington Interscholastic Activities Association since competition between member schools and non-member schools was prohibited.

Chapter 5

Athletic Issues

INTRODUCTION

There are many legal issues affecting today's sports administrator. This chapter reviews those issues, in particular coaching issues, disclosure, and sex discrimination.

There is one underlying management failure in most liability cases: poor, ignored, or false communication. The *United States v. Reliance Insurance Co.* case is a good example of the multiple legal consequences resulting from failure to properly communicate. Failure to communicate led to the filing of the case; the ignored or intended failure to communicate contractual changes added to the number and types of liabilities; and, failure to communicate affected the liabilities of more than just the contracting parties. The *Reliance* case is an example for administrators to recognize the pitfalls of poor communication.

A surety agent is released from the obligations of a bonded contract for the Army-Navy game.

UNITED STATES V. RELIANCE INSURANCE CO.
799 F2d 1382
United States Court of Appeals, 9th Circuit
September 16, 1986

FACTS. The Army-Navy '83 Foundation was organized to bring the 1983 Army-Navy football game to the Rose Bowl in Pasadena, California.

The Foundation agreed to pay Army and Navy $875,000 each from television and gate revenues; also, each contestant was to receive up to $100,000 for any additional expenses. In addition, the Foundation was to pay for the travel, room, and board of the cadets and midshipmen to Pasadena.

The Foundation, per the agreement, obtained two bonds from Reliance to guarantee their obligation for ticket sales and concessions, and to cover the additional expenses. Reliance issued the bonds upon the assurance by the Foundation that television proceeds would be assigned to pay the face amount of the bonds. That assignment was never made.

Subsequent to the bond issuance, the Foundation modified its agreement with Army and Navy:

1. the date of the game was changed to accommodate television;

2. per NCAA regulations, television proceeds were to be paid directly to the contestants, not to the Foundation; and

3. in exchange for Foundation's waiver of its rights to ticket revenues, Army and Navy agreed to pay for the transportation, and room and board for the cadets and midshipmen.

Reliance was never informed of the modifications to the agreement. When Foundation failed to pay Army and Navy for the additional expenses incurred and guaranteed under the second bond, the service academies filed a lawsuit to recover the additional expenses from Reliance. The court ruled in favor of Reliance based on the material alterations to the original bonded contract.

ISSUE. Did the modifications to the contract between Foundation and Army and Navy materially change the bonded contract to the prejudice of Reliance?

DECISION. If the bonded contract is *materially* altered or changed without the surety's consent, the surety is discharged from liability. The key to this bond was that Foundation's funds consisted of ticket, concession, and television revenues. Those proceeds were the only means the Foundation had to meet its obligations, including cost of the bonds. When Foundation waived its rights to the ticket revenues, it materially altered the position of Reliance which might have declined to issue the bonds, absent the right to the revenues.

Without proof by Army and Navy that Reliance knew of and consented to the modifications, Reliance cannot be held to have waived or ratified the modifications.

COACHING ISSUES

We have examined liability issues affecting the safety and care of recreation patrons, users, and guests. In Chapter Six, "Workmens' Compensation," we will examine the liability issues affecting employees and their job-related stresses. From the standpoint of athletic management, however, perhaps the person who has the most impact on a sports program is the athletic coach. The coach holds a unique niche in the world of sports management since his or her role is usually one of middle management; yet, in many instances, it is afforded greater notoriety, freedom, and benefits than the top management. By the same token, the price that coaches must pay for that recognition is the uncertainty and instability of producing successful, competitive athletic programs.

High School Coaches

A growing concern in interscholastic athletics is the appointment of non-certificated coaches. A number of states have recently moved to allow non-teaching personnel to assume coaching positions either because of budget constraints, or the unavailability of qualified, certificated personnel. School boards face many potential liabilities for hiring non-certificated coaching personnel, beginning with the hiring practice itself.

The qualifications of a high school varsity basketball coach may be settled by arbitration.

ENLARGED CITY SCHOOL DISTRICT OF TROY V. TROY
TEACHERS ASSOCIATION
508 N.E.2d 930
Court of Appeals of New York
April 23, 1987

FACTS. The Enlarged City School District and the Troy Teachers Association (New York) entered into a collective bargaining agreement for the 1983 to 1986 school years. As part of the agreement, the school district agreed that any vacancies occurring in instructional positions during the term of the agreement would be filled from the association membership.

When the district hired a non-association member for the part-time position of head varsity basketball coach at Troy High School, the teachers association filed a grievance. They alleged that two members of their unit had applied for the position, each a previous head basketball coach at the high school. The district's position was that the two applicants were unqualified, and denied the grievance.

The association demanded arbitration under the collective bargaining agreement. The school district filed this lawsuit requesting that the court stop the arbitration proceedings on public policy grounds. The court refused to grant the district's request.

ISSUE. The school district maintained that an arbitration decision might require the district to hire an unqualified person although the district is supposed to be the ultimate judge of a person's qualifications. Does the school district have to risk a potentially adverse arbitration order?

DECISION. The court ruled that the district's request was premature although the public policy argument of the district may be correct. Since the arbitrator had not issued a decision, it could not be assumed that the arbitrator would substitute his judgment for that of the district regarding personnel qualifications.

> "To justify preemptive judicial intervention in the arbitration process, public policy considerations embodied in decisional law or statutes must 'prohibit, in an absolute sense, particular matters being decided or certain relief being granted by an arbitrator'." (p. 931)

The interscholastic coach has traditionally enjoyed the *in loco parentis* status of educators, that immunity protected supervisory and discipline-related functions. Yet, it appears that the primary source of litigation affecting coaches remains their supervision of student-athletes. Although the coach may be held to the duty of ordinary, prudent care in furnishing athletes with safe equipment, it is the supervision of those athletes and the coach's own conduct which pose the greatest liability problem. Recently, the coach's authority to discipline has been limited by a number of factors;[1] however, the coach still has parental rights when it comes to the supervision of athletes during practice or competition. The coach's supervisory duties take many forms. In *Broward County School Baord v. Ruiz*, the court examined the areas of supervision; in *Beckett v. Clinton Prairie School Corporation*, the court reviewed the coaching supervision.

A coach's primary duty of supervision is for his team.

BROWARD COUNTY SCHOOL BOARD V. RUIZ
493 So.2d 474
District Court of Appeal of Florida
July 2, 1986

FACTS. A Hallandale High School (Florida) Junior Varsity football player returned to the school cafeteria after a team photo session. While waiting for a ride home with his father, he was severly beaten by three other students. His coach had remained on the practice field with other members of the team. There were no security or supervisory personnel in the cafeteria at the time of the attack.

The student filed a lawsuit against the school for its failure to provide adequate supervision and safety. He was awarded $30,000 by a jury.

ISSUE. Did the junior varsity coach have a duty of care to the student? Did the school have a duty of care to the student? Is the school or the coach liable for injuries caused by other students?

DECISION. The junior varsity coach did not have a duty of care or supervision to the young athlete because his primary duty of supervision lay with his players who were on the field, and not to a single player in the cafeteria.

However, the *school* did owe a duty of supervision and safety to the student, especially during after school hours when the opportunity for student misconduct was greatest. Since the cafeteria was the place where students congregated while waiting for rides, it was a likely place for student misconduct to occur.

A baseball coach violates the requisite duty of care to players when he disregards written coaching instructions.

BECKETT V. CLINTON PRAIRIE SCHOOL CORPORATION
504 N.E.2d 552
Supreme Court of Indiana
February 27, 1987

FACTS. The assistant baseball coach at Clinton Prairie High School (Indiana) conducted a drill where he hit fly balls to a designated outfielder; the outfielder would then throw the ball to a cutoff man. Clinton Prairie's baseball program had a *written* rule, and coached the players, that outfielders had preference over infielders in fielding fly balls.

During the practice, the coach hit a fly ball that the plaintiff, an outfielder, called for; however, the coach instructed the cutoff man to make the catch. The outfielder did not hear the coach's instruction to the cutoff man. And, due to wind conditions, neither the coach nor the cutoff man heard the plaintiff call for the ball. The plaintiff collided with the cutoff man and was severely injured.

The plaintiff's lawsuit against Clinton Prairie for failure to warn, inadequate supervision, and other causes was dismissed.

ISSUE. Did the assistant baseball coach breach a duty of care to the plaintiff? Did the plaintiff incur the risk of injury by collision with the cutoff man?

DECISION. Clinton Prairie contended the only duty it owed to the plaintiff was to refrain from wilful, deliberate, or reckless conduct; and that it owed less of a duty to a high school student than it would if the plaintiff was a younger student. The court established the standard of care owed was that of an ordinary, prudent person under the same or similar conditions.

The coach called for the cutoff man to make the catch despite the written rule of outfielder preference, and he did not appreciate that he might not be heard due to wind conditions. Therefore, his actions did not conform to the requisite degree of care owed to the players.

However, the court upheld dismissal of the case because it found that the plaintiff incurred the risk of injury, which is: ". . .the conscious, deliberate and intentional embarkation upon the course of conduct with knowledge of the circumstances." The court determined that the plaintiff knew or was aware collisions do occur as a risk in baseball, and voluntarily incurred that risk.

College Coaches

In today's litigious society, with the move away from teaching certification for coaches, there is an accelerating move for their competency certification. This awareness would enhance coaching competency levels and liability protection. However, the competency certification concept is more relevant to youth and interscholastic sports. The primary qualification for collegiate and professional coaches remains the success of the specified athletic program.

Two companion cases (*Lindsey v. Dempsey* and *Lindsey v. Clossco*) relating to the termination of a basketball coach at the University of Arizona presented two issues for litigation: first, if the recommendation by an athletic director to terminate a coach constituted interference with the coach's contract; and second, if termination of the coach cancelled his contract with a shoe company.

An athletic director's recommendation to fire a coach does not constitute intentional interference with contractual relations.

LINDSEY V. DEMPSEY
735 P.2d 840
Court of Appeals of Arizona
January 27, 1987

FACTS. The plaintiff was hired as the head basketball coach at the University of Arizona in April, 1983. A new athletic director was hired two months later. In June, 1984, the plaintiff was fired upon the recommendation of the athletic director.

The plaintiff filed a lawsuit against the athletic director, alleging that the athletic director intentionally interfered with the coach's contract with the university, and intentionally inflicted emotional distress upon the plaintiff. The case was dismissed.

ISSUE. The elements of the tort of intentional interference with contractual relations are: (1) existence of a contract, (2) knowledge of the relationship or expectancy on the part of the interferer, (3) intentional interference which induces or causes a breach or termination of the contract, (4) damage to the party who has been interfered with, and, (5) improper motive or means by the interferer.

The tort of intentional infliction of emotional distress requires intentional, extreme, and outrageous conduct which causes severe emotional distress.

How did the court view the conduct of the athletic director?

DECISION. The court ruled that there was no evidence of the fifth element of intentional interference, that is, that the athletic director's actions were improper as to motive or means. The coach contended that he had an implied four-year agreement, but that he was considered a temporary coach by the athletic director until a "big-name" coach could be hired. However, the evidence disclosed that the athletic director met with the coach several times regarding personal and coaching problems, met with the basketball team once, and had listened to reports from other persons regarding coaching problems.

There was no evidence that the athletic director intended to ruin the plaintiff's coaching career as alleged. And, contrary to the plaintiff's argument that he was just a "tool" until a big-name coach could be hired, the evidence showed that the decision to terminate the plaintiff occurred prior to the search for a new coach. Accordingly, there was nothing to suggest that the athletic director's conduct was outrageous, or that there was any intentional infliction of emotional distress.

"(The plaintiff) has not cited us to anything in the record which indicates (the athletic director) acted other than in his capacity as (the plaintiff's) supervisor, and as athletic director responsible for, among other things, the success of the University's basketball program." (p. 843)

Firing a college basketball coach is a condition subsequent which extinguishes the coach's agreement with a shoe distributor.

LINDSEY V. CLOSSCO
642 F.Supp. 250
United States District Court, D. Arizona
July 30, 1986

FACTS. The plaintiff was hired by the University of Arizona as men's basketball coach prior to the 1982-1983 season. He was contacted by representatives of Adidas shoe manufacturers regarding a contract for his "advisory and consulting" services for $30,000 a year. The terms of the agreed contract included his commitment to encourage the Arizona basketball players to wear Adidas shoes.

In January, 1983, he was paid $5,000 as an advance on another year's contract. However, he was fired as basketball coach in March, 1983; Adidas immediately terminated the agreement. The plaintiff sued Adidas for the remaining balance due under the anticipated second contract. The court ruled, however, that his termination by the University of Arizona extinguished his agreement with Adidas.

ISSUE. What was the legal effect of the termination by Arizona on the agreement with Adidas?

DECISION.

> "A condition subsequent refers to a future event, upon the happening of which the obligation is no longer binding on the other party, if he chooses to avail himself of the condition." (p. 255)

The coach's termination was a "condition subsequent" which extinguished the shoe distributor's obligation to perform under the second contract. The nature of the agreement was such that the promotion of Adidas shoes could be effectively performed by the coach only in his role as basketball coach.

As discussed, a winning program is the price most coaches must pay in order to enjoy the privileges of the coaching ranks. The pressures for quick success on the collegiate level can be devastating, as demonstrated in *Lather v. Huron College*.

A college basketball coach is not eligible for workmen's compensation benefits for mental disabilities leading to attempted suicide.

LATHER V. HURON COLLEGE
413 N.W.2d 369
Supreme Court of South Dakota
September 30, 1987

FACTS. The claimant was hired as the basketball coach at Huron College (South Dakota). The court found that, during his six month tenure, equipment was stolen; six of his 14 players were found academically ineligible; he did not have enough players to scrimmage (he played one game with only five players); one player threatened him with a knife; a number of players were involved in drinking escapades; he had a number of players who resented the fact he refused to sign their work time sheets because they had not performed their work; the president of the school did not actively support his discipline procedures; his office was a leaking, unfurnished storage area; he had to arrange a holiday tournament though he was totally inexperienced; and, his team was having a losing season.

He began experiencing severe symptoms of mental illness. Ultimately, he attempted suicide by throwing himself from a car traveling at approximately 60 miles per hour. His claim for workmen's compensation benefits was denied.

ISSUE. Are mental disabilities produced solely by gradual mental stress compensable injuries under workmen's compensation?

DECISION. The court, while noting its sensitivity to mental illness or disabilities induced by mental stress, stated that it could not find anything that would indicate legislative intent, express or implied, to provide benefits for this type of case.

A dissenting opinion noted that most jurisdictions would award benefits. Further, the key to mental disability cases was whether the stress to which the employee succumbed was greater than the stress encountered by most employees in their everyday work life. Added to that, the coach's attending physician did state that the employment at Huron College was a sufficient cause of the resulting mental illness.

In the *Reliance* case, Army and Navy lost expense monies because of poor or missed communication. Similarly, in *Bruner v. University of Southern Mississippi*, the job negotiations for an assistant coaching position became entangled in a web of misunderstanding and false assumption.

A head football coach does not have the authority to contract with an applicant for an assistant coaching position.

BRUNER V. UNIVERSITY OF SOUTHERN MISSISSIPPI
501 So.2d 1113
Supreme Court of Mississippi
January 28, 1987

FACTS. The plaintiff, an applicant for the position of assistant football coach at the University of Southern Mississippi, met with the head football coach and the athletic director. The head coach told the plaintiff that he was his choice for the job; the athletic director told the plaintiff that he was the recommended choice for the position. The plaintiff was further advised that his formal approval was pending before the University Board of Trustees. Acting on the assumption that he was going to be hired, the plaintiff and his family made their preparations to move to the university.

The plaintiff was then informed by the athletic director and the head football coach that he was not going to be hired. The plaintiff sued the university, the athletic director, and the head football coach for breach of contract. The cases against the university and the athletic director were dismissed; the jury returned a verdict in favor of the head football coach.

ISSUE. Did the head football coach have the authority to offer an employment contract to the plaintiff?

DECISION. The University of Southern Mississippi operated under authority granted by the state legislature. The legislature enacted a statute that permitted only the board of trustees to contract with employees. The only authority of university employees was to nominate parties for positions, subject to approval by the trustees. In this case, there were no minutes or records indicating the plaintiff had even been nominated. Thus, there was not a valid employment contract. The plaintiff learned that when dealing with an apparent agent, a party is at his or her own risk regarding the extent of that agent's authority to contract.

The court also affirmed the jury's judgment that provision of an automobile, use of office keys, and access to game films were actions consistent with the treatment afforded to all applicants, not just the plaintiff.

DISCLOSURE

The NCAA's role and rule of confidentiality in its investigative processes has been the subject of constitutional claims. When the claim is for disclosure of the budgets and documents of private universities and athletic corporations, the potential for conflict of interest arises.

Private institutions usually are not subject to compulsory disclosure unless they perform a governmental or "state" function, or if they receive federal funding assistance. Publicly-funded universities and colleges are subject to the legal process of constitutional claims. Athletic associations, such as the NCAA, also are subject to constitutional process since their role is perceived as the regulative body, with governmental authority, over athletics.

There has been a conservative shift in recent years regarding the legal standing of private institutions. The courts are disregarding the public regulation of private schools, public revenues for private schools, or the performance of a public function (education) by private schools as determinative factors subjecting private institutions to the legal processes of disclosure.

In *A. H. Belo v. Southern Methodist University* and *Macon Telegraph Publishing Co. v. Board of Regents of University System of Georgia*, the courts considered whether two different state open records laws required the compulsory disclosure of NCAA investigative documents. Specifically, in *Belo*, the court examined the legal status of the athletics-generated revenues produced by private schools;[2] however, in *Macon Telegraph* the court decided that a private corporation that administered the athletic program of a state-supported university was, in fact, a public agency.

Athletic revenues generated from gate receipts and broadcast rights are not public funds for purposes of invoking the Texas Open Records Act.

A. H. BELO V. SOUTHERN METHODIST UNIVERSITY
734 S.W.2d 720
Court of Appeals of Texas
July 13, 1987

FACTS. The Dallas Morning News filed a suit under the Texas Open Records Act (TORA) requesting that the member universities of the Southwest Athletic Conference (SWC) be required to turn over all documents relating to the 1983-1985 investigation by the NCAA, the SWC, and the schools themselves. The four private university members countered that they were not governmental bodies subject to the TORA provisions.

The newspaper's suit was dismissed when the court agreed that Southern Methodist, Rice, Baylor, and Texas Christian universities were not subject to the act.

ISSUE. The Texas Open Records Act defines a governmental body as:

> "the part, section, or portion of every organization, corporation, commission, committee, institution, or agency which is supported in whole or in part by public funds, or which expends public funds..." (p. 723)

Are the private universities supported by public funds?

DECISION. Public funds are "funds of the State of Texas or any governmental subdivision thereof." Therefore, the focus was whether or not public funds were used to support the private universities' athletic programs.

The athletic revenues generated by the SWC universities were from gate receipts and broadcast rights. The disbursement of those funds was made by a pre-arranged plan of the Southwest Athletic Conference. A portion of the funds were retained by each university. The remaining funds were paid to the SWC to fund its budget. Any funds in excess of the SWC budget were then divided equally among the member schools.

The court ruled the schools, in effect, were acting as conduits or collection agents for SWC purposes, and the monies forwarded by the SWC to the private schools were contractual payments. Accordingly, the court concluded the funds were not public monies, and the private schools were not governmental bodies since they were not supported by public funds.

Budget documents of the Georgia Athletic Association, a private corporation, are public records.

MACON TELEGRAPH PUBLISHING CO. V. BOARD OF
REGENTS OF UNIVERSITY
SYSTEM OF GEORGIA
350 S.E.2d 23
Supreme Court of Georgia
November 19, 1986

FACTS. The Macon Telegraph Publishing Company filed a lawsuit to compel the Georgia Athletic Association to produce documents disclosing its income, expenses, assets, and liabilities. Under Georgia law, the Georgia Athletic Association was a private corporation charged with administering the athletic program at the University of Georgia. Further, the Georgia law stated, in part:

" . . .such athletic associations are not agencies of the state and are not subject to the same limitations and restrictions which might apply if they were state agencies." (p. 24)

However, the Georgia Supreme Court ruled that association documents were public records within the meaning of Georgia's Open Records Act, and were subject to public disclosure.

ISSUE. If the Georgia Athletic Association is to be treated, by state law, as a private corporation and not a state agency, how can its documents be considered public records?

DECISION. The administration of intercollegiate athletics at the University of Georgia is a legitimate function of the university, a public agency.

The president of the university is charged with the authority to manage the athletic program; he uses the Georgia Athletic Association as the management tool to carry out that function. The vice president of business and finance for the university, under the direction of the president, serves as treasurer for the association, and is in control of documents relating to income, expenses, assets, and liabilities.

Therefore, documents "prepared and maintained in the course of the operation of a public office are public records," within the meaning of the Open Records Act.

There are interesting implications to the *Belo* case. If it is accepted that the athletic revenues of a private institution are not public monies for disclosure purposes, yet the NCAA is performing a "state action" in its regulation of intercollegiate athletics, it seems axiomatic that the NCAA cannot truly represent the interests of its private school members in litigation relating to its rule of investigative confidentiality.[3]

DISCRIMINATION

There are a number of laws defining sex discrimination. In athletics, three of the primary sources are state Equal Rights Amendments, Title IX, and Title VII protections. This section examines recent case law involving each of those three sources.

The allocation of a collegiate athletic department's budget for women's programs remains a heated issue; a disproportionate share of athletic monies and scholarships is one of the first indices of discrimination. In *Blair v. Washington State University*, which was filed for the alleged violation of the state Equal Rights Amendment, the court was called upon to measure those demonstrable indicators.

Football revenues cannot be excluded from calculation of university support to athletics in a sex discrimination action.

BLAIR V. WASHINGTON STATE UNIVERSITY
740 P.2d 1379
Supreme Court of Washington
August 6, 1987

FACTS. Female student-athletes and coaches at Washington State University filed a discrimination suit against the university under the state Equal Rights Amendment. The evidence showed that total funding available for women's programs was 23 percent of that available for men's programs, that there had been a large increase in the number of participation opportunities for men while opportunities for women decreased during the same period of time, and that the budget for men's scholarships had increased.

The trial court found there was discriminatory treatment of females by the athletic department, and ordered that the university allocate 37.5 percent of the university's financial support to intercollegiate athletics for the women's programs. However, its order also stated that football was excluded from the calculation of university support for opportunities, scholarships, and distribution of funds, and that each sport would retain its own sports-generated funds. The Washington Supreme Court reversed the exclusion of football from the university support calculation, but agreed that each sport would retain its own funds.

ISSUE. Should football be treated as a unique function to university athletics due to its ability to generate revenues, number of participants, and other distinguishing characteristics?

DECISION. The court noted that the overall operation of the athletic program discriminated against the female student-athletes and coaches. Since football was an essential part of that athletic program, to exclude it from the calculation of the university funding process for athletics would only further aggravate the discriminatory policies that had occurred.

The court ruled, however, that each sport should be entitled to retain its own sports-generated revenues as an incentive to expand those revenues, and to fund respective sports from those revenues, rather than from legislative appropriations.

The *Blair* decision probably left the plaintiffs and the defendants miffed. From the perspective of the female athletes and coaches, the exclusion of specific football-generated revenues foreclosed those assets from distribution to women's programs. From the perspective of the university, the inclusion of the football program in the calculation of university support produced a dramatic impact on the budgeting priorities for athletics. The greatest impact, however, was that revenue-producing sports were not going to be treated distinctly, once discrimination was established.

Even with the additional provisions of Title IX protection, female athletes may be hard-pressed to enjoy the affirmative protection granted by the law. Obviously, the first and foremost problem is to invoke the Title IX jurisdiction. Although that jurisdiction relies on federal assistance to institutions and their programs, the type of assistance is not easily defined.

The continued approach of the courts is that Title IX is "program-specific." That was the result of the now-famous *Grove City* case where the court ruled that legal review in discrimination suits was limited to the identification of specific programs or departments which were recipients of federal financial assistance.[4] *Bennett v. West Texas State University*, filed before the *Grove City* decision, reflects the attitude of many courts regarding the program-specific effect of Title IX claims.

Federal education assistance to student-athletes does not constitute sufficient indirect aid to invoke title IX coverage.

BENNETT V. WEST TEXAS STATE UNIVERSITY
799 F.2d 155
United States Court of Appeals, Fifth Circuit
September 5, 1986

FACTS. Six female student-athletes filed a sex discrimination lawsuit against West Texas State University. They alleged they were denied equal opportunity in the university's athletic programs citing disproportionate allocation of the budget, scholarships, and facilities. They appealed the lower court decision that the athletic department was not federally-assisted within the meaning of Title IX.

ISSUE. The student-athletes contended:

1. there is receipt of federal education assistance funds by West Texas State which *directly* benefits the athletic department;

2. the sex discrimination in the athletic department "infected" the other federally-assisted programs in the university; and

3. the administrative duties of the student financial aid office in processing athletic scholarships constitutes indirect receipt of federal funds benefitting athletics.

DECISION. To support a Title IX claim, the student-athletes needed to show that the athletic department was a direct or indirect recipient of federal funds. They were unable to prove their first contention that there was direct receipt of funds. The court concentrated on the allegation that the university was an indirect recipient of federal funds, and ruled:

1. federal education assistance grants and scholarships for students might have a "trickle down" effect, but it is difficult, if not impossible, to determine which university programs derive any benefit;

2. athletics is a "discrete" program which does not affect the university's academic structure, so the theory that the alleged sex discrimination in the athletic program also pervades other federally-assisted programs (the "infection" theory) fails; and

3. athletic scholarships are awarded solely by the athletic department. The role of the student financial aid office is ministerial in regard to athletic scholarships, and not sufficient to invoke Title IX coverage.

Title VII offers protection to persons, employed by agencies receiving federal funds, who are terminated as a result of sex or other suspect discrimination. However, as evidenced by *Gray v. University of Arkansas*, the proof required of a sex discrimination claimant can be burdensome.

A female academic coordinator fails to prove Title VII discrimination in her discharge by the University of Arkansas Athletic Department.

GRAY V. UNIVERSITY OF ARKANSAS
658 F.Supp. 709
U.S. District Court, W.D. Arkansas
April 20, 1987

FACTS. A female academic coordinator for the University of Arkansas Athletic Department was terminated on the recommendation of the head football coach. Her lawsuit alleging sex discrimination under Title VII was dismissed.

ISSUE. What are the legal burdens and obligations of the female and the employer in a sex discrimination case?

DECISION. The female must first establish a prima facie case of discrimination, that is, that the employer's reasons for the discharge are not very substantial. After the plaintiff has met that burden, the employer must be able to "articulate a legitimate non-discriminatory reason" for the discharge. The plaintiff then has the opportunity to establish that the employer's proffered reasons for the discharge were "pretextual." Pretextual means that the reasons given were not legitimate or non-discriminatory, but were a sham to cover the real discriminatory motive.

In this case, the plaintiff established a prima facie case, but the court upheld the employer's reasons for the discharge on the basis that an employer retains the right to choose an employee based on a "feeling," or any other reason that is not impermissible by law.

> "The court believes that the reasons given, as delineated above, for her termination were not pretextual. The fact that they may not be 'very good' is not sufficient. This court must believe, and it simply does not, that they were not only 'not good reasons,' but that they were given to hide the true state of affairs." (p. 725)

The plaintiff bears the burden, at all times, of proving the discrimination by a preponderance of the evidence. In other words, after viewing the evidence in its entirety, the plaintiff must convince the court that *more likely than not* she was terminated because of her sex.

ADDITIONAL ISSUES

This section examines legal concepts which limit tort liability in sports and protect sports revenues.

Limited Liability

Workmen's Compensation. Chapter Six, "Workmen's Compensation", examines the liability an employer has to his or her employees who suffer job-related injuries. In many states, professional athletes are eligible for medical, wage, and disability benefits awarded under workmen's compensation. However, workmen's compensation is an exclusive remedy. There is not a right to a tort remedy against the employer unless the athlete-employee was intentionally injured by the employer. It is very difficult for an employee to establish such an intent. In *DePiano v. Montreal Baseball Club, Ltd.*, a minor league baseball player unsuccessfully argued that he was intentionally injured by the ball club when he was required to play hurt (resulting in the premature end of his career) and because the team trainer improperly treated his injury.

Failure to provide timely medical care to an injured baseball player is not intentional misconduct.

DePIANO V. MONTREAL BASEBALL CLUB, LTD.
663 F.Supp. 116
United States District Court, W.D. Pennsylvania
July 8, 1987

FACTS. Plaintiff, a minor league baseball player in the Montreal organization, was injured when he chased a long fly ball into an outfield wall. He filed a lawsuit against the defendant alleging that he was not afforded timely medical treatment and care for his shoulder injury; and, that he was required to play ball despite the injury. The aggravated condition led to the early end of his career.

His claim was rejected when the court ruled that the player's only remedy was an action in Workmen's Compensation.

ISSUE. The New York Workmens' Compensation statute provided that intentional injuries were exceptions to its exclusive coverage. Plaintiff alleged that defendant's conduct regarding his injury was intentionally directed to harm him. Since the treatment of his injury was left to the team trainer; and, since he was required to play because the team was short of outfielders, was the defendant's conduct an intentional harm, and basis for a negligence suit?

DECISION. The intentional harm exception requires proof that the employer committed an intentional or deliberate act directed at causing harm to the specific employee. The court noted that knowledge and appreciation of a risk of danger alone were not sufficient proof of an intentional injury.

The court believed the player had a basis for proving negligent conduct on the part of the defendant. However, negligent conduct was not sufficient to meet the intentional harm exception. Also, proof that he was required to play due to a shortage of players provided the employer with a motive for its actions which belied any conduct intended to intentionally injure the plaintiff.

The work relationship between a college athlete and his or her school is often litigated. Generally, it is recognized that athletes are not employees of their colleges; thus, they are ineligible for workmen's compensation benefits for their injuries. The failure to recognize athletes as university employees also served to bar the claim of an athlete "intentionally" injured during a basketball game in *Townsend v. State of California.* The plaintiff did not seek workmen's compensation, but his claim was rejected as a result of it.

A university student-athlete is not an employee.

TOWNSEND V. STATE OF CALIFORNIA
237 Cal. Rptr. 146
Court of Appeal 2nd District
May 21, 1987

FACTS. A basketball player at San Jose State University struck the plaintiff, a basketball player from UCLA, with his fists during a game between the two schools. The plaintiff sued the defendant, the state of California, San Jose State University, its basketball coach and athletic director. The jury returned a verdict of $25,000 against the San Jose State player. But, the court dismissed the case against the other parties.

The plaintiff's appeal that San Jose State was liable for damages because defendant was an employee was rejected.

ISSUE. The plaintiff contended that the San Jose State player was an employee under the doctrine of respondeat superior. Under that legal concept, an employer is liable for the damages caused by an employee.

DECISION. The court stated that any liability to be imposed upon the state depended on the applicability of the California Tort Claims Act. Generally, public agencies are not liable for any damages, although the court examined an exception that attached liability for certain acts of public agency employees made in the course of their employment.

Since the doctrine of respondeat superior depends on a master-servant (employment) relationship, the court attempted to determine whether a college athlete met the definition of employee for purposes of the Tort Claims Act, or the requirements of the doctrine.

The court relied on California workmen's compensation language, which specifically excluded amateur student-athletes from the definition of employee. The court ruled that the San Jose State player was not an employee, thus his conduct did not impose liability on the state or its supervisory employees for his actions.

Releases. Auto racing is unique to sport, and sport law, for a number of reasons. It is a professional racing activity that is unhampered by the burdens of legalized gambling; its regulation is limited to the safety and pleasure of its participants and fans. Also, it holds some inherent dangers for its spectators so it is legally affected by assumed or incurred risks. Therefore, in few sports are signed releases of liability as finely scrutinized as those in auto racing.

Executed release of liability is a valid defense against the negligence claim of a spectator injured at a car race.

VALLEY NATIONAL BANK V. N.A.S.C.A.R.
736 P.2d 1186
Court of Appeals of Arizona
March 12, 1987

FACTS. The plaintiff, an experienced professional race car driver and former member of the National Association of Stock Car Auto Racing (NASCAR), attended a stock car race with his wife. Though never a participant, his wife had extensive experience with car racing.

During the NASCAR-sanctioned race, the plaintiff and his wife entered the pit area of the track, usually reserved only for drivers. The track personnel generally did not ask parties entering the pit area if they were spectators. However, if they were so identified, they were re-directed to the general admission area. Drivers were allowed to enter the pit area only after signing three documents represented as releases of liability. Neither the plaintiff nor his wife were asked if they were drivers or spectators; they entered the pit area after signing the releases. The plaintiff's wife suffered severe brain injuries when two race cars collided and struck a trailer near where she was seated.

The plaintiff's lawsuit against the track was dismissed when the signed releases of liability were ruled to be valid.

ISSUE. The plaintiff alleged that he and his wife had not read the releases since they were without their reading glasses. Further, had they understood they were giving up their right to sue in the case of defendant's negligence, they would not have entered the pit area.

A valid release must not be contrary to public policy, and its terms must be clearly understood by the party giving up the right to recover. Why were the waivers deemed to be valid in this case?

DECISION. There was nothing contrary to public policy in this case since the plaintiff's wife was not required to be in the pit area, and because car racing is not affected with any public policy interest.

The court rejected the plaintiff's appeal since there was conflicting evidence regarding whether the terms of the releases were understood. Additionally, the form, content, and language of the releases left little doubt what the documents were, or whether they had been voluntarily executed.

Finally, the court rejected the claim that the releases were invalid because they were intended for drivers, not spectators. The court reasoned that the plaintiffs implicitly represented they were not spectators when they signed the releases, and they could not now assert otherwise.

Sports Revenues

In many liability cases, juries are instructed to consider the plaintiff's loss of potential earnings as proper damage. The computation of a potential earning often requires a great deal of speculation. However, the compensation for potential economic loss remains a recognized legal remedy. One of the few exceptions is gaming events, as in *Youst v. Longo*.

"In light of these important public policies, we conclude that a cause of action will not lie for prospective economic loss which arises between competitors during a sporting contest." (p. 738)

YOUST V. LONGO
729 P.2d 728
Supreme Court of California
January 2, 1987

FACTS. The plaintiff owned a trotter named Bat Champ. He alleged that the defendant, who was driving a horse named The Thilly Brudder, intentionally drove his horse into the path of Bat Champ; and struck Bat Champ with his whip causing the horse to break stride. Bat Champ finished sixth in the race at Hollywood Park, and The Thilly Brudder finished second.

The plaintiff unsuccessfully sued the defendant for the difference in the amount of prize money between Bat Champ's sixth place finish and the amount Bat Champ would have won but for the interference.

ISSUE. The California Supreme Court stated:

"Is a racehorse owner entitled to tort damages when the harness driver of another horse negligently or intentionally interferes with the owner's horse during a race, thereby preventing the owner from the chance of winning a particular cash prize?" (p.730)

DECISION.

". . .tort liability for interference with prospective economic advantage is not available, as a matter of law and *public policy*, in the context of a sporting event." (p. 732)

It is recognized that business interests may be protected by expectancies. However, there is no compelling reason to extend any such protection to the outcome of a sporting contest with its high degree of uncertainty.

In a related issue, the California Horse Racing Board was recognized as a regulatory and disciplinary agency. However, there is neither express nor implicit authorization for the board to award compensatory or punitive tort damages to the victims of rules violations.

"Ticket-scalping" is traditionally considered a shady, "back alley" activity. Recently, it has achieved its own type of glamour; many sporting events are promoted, unofficially, by the amounts scalpers are able to get for 50-yard line, box seat, or mid-court tickets. In *People v. Trabucchi*, the court upheld a state criminal law which prohibited the sale of baseball tickets, without the permission of the baseball team, for more than box office price.

Michigan statute prohibiting ticket scalping is constitutional.

PEOPLE V. TRABUCCHI
408 N.W.2d 563
Court of Appeals of Michigan
June 16, 1987

FACTS. The defendant, operating as Metropolitan Ticket Service, regularly purchased tickets from the Detroit Tigers. The ticket service sponsored bus trips to baseball games, and the name of the ticket service was regularly displayed at Tiger Stadium in appreciation for its patronage. The defendant was charged with a criminal offense for violating Michigan's "ticket scalping" statute because he was selling Tiger tickets for $3.00 more than box office price.

The defendant argued that the ticket scalping law was unconstitutional because it delegated legislative authority to private individuals. That is, under the statute, his actions were unlawful; yet, another ticket service was selling Tiger tickets for $.65 over box office price and was not in violation of the statute because it had a written agreement with the Tigers. Since the Tigers had the choice to give or not to give permission for these sales, the defendant concluded the Tigers were ultimately left to decide whether or not an act was a criminal act. The court disagreed and ruled the statute was constitutional.

ISSUE. Private individuals do not have the power to make laws determining what is lawful or unlawful conduct. If the Tigers allow one ticket company to sell tickets at a price above box office price, should the defendant's actions be considered criminal activity because he sells tickets over box office price without their permission?

DECISION. It is important to distinguish that this case involved a criminal prosecution, not a civil case for damages. The defendant's argument reflected the concern that a private individual may not determine what is lawful conduct in criminal law.

The defendant believed the Tigers agreement with the other ticket company modified the language of the criminal statute. However, the court said the Tigers did not determine whether a ticket seller was violating the statute, rather they only decided who had permission to sell the tickets at the higher price. When permission to sell was denied, it was the ticket seller who decided whether or not he would abide with that denial, or would violate the statute.

There was dissent to the decision by a judge who noted that permission to sell tickets at a higher price still was conditioned by the promoter's own interest, not measurable by constitutional standards for criminal law.

REFERENCES

Appenzeller, H. 1975. *Athletics and the Law*. Charlottesville, VA: The Michie Company.

Berry, R. and G. Wong. 1986 *Law and Business of the Sports Industries*. Vol. II. Dover, MA: Auburn House Publishing Company.

Schubert, G., R.K. Smith, and J.C. Trentadue. 1986. *Sports Law*. St. Paul, MN: West Publishing Co.

[1] In *Alabama State Tenure Commission v. Birmingham Board of Education*, 500 So.2d 1155 (Ala. Civ. App. 1986), the Court of Civil Appeals upheld the cancellation of the employment contract of a tenured physical educator and coach who was found to have inflicted corporal punishment on his players in violation of Alabama law. In addition, he conducted basketball practices contrary to the rules of the Alabama High School Athletic Association. The court overruled the State Tenure Commission, and affirmed the decision of the Board of Education that the coach's conduct constituted "immorality, incompetency, and other good and just causes" for cancellation of his contract.

[2] In Chapter Two, we reviewed the decision in *Greenhill v. Carpenter*, 718 S.W.2d 268 (Tenn. Ct. App. 1986), wherein the Tennessee Court of Appeals ruled that athletic department revenues generated from non-tax sources were public funds since Tennessee educational institutions and departments were state agencies for purposes of governmental immunity.

[3] See *Kneeland v. National Collegiate Athletic Association*, 806 F.2d 1285 (5th Cir., 1987): private universities, Rice and SMU, were not allowed to defend their privacy interests in a related disclosure suit filed against the NCAA. The court ruled the NCAA adequately represented the interests of its members.

[4] In *Grove City College v. Bell*, 465 U.S. 555, 104 S.Ct. 104 (1984), the United States Supreme Court rejected the claim that federal educational assistance to students at Grove City College, a private school, benefitted all the programs at the college. The court ruled that the assistance was program-specific to the student financial aid program. Therefore, federal assistance could be terminated for that program if the college refused to comply with Title IX reports, but no sanctions could be imposed on the school's other programs.

Chapter 6

Workmen's Compensation

INTRODUCTION

Workmen's compensation is a timely subject because of the impact employee fitness has for today's recreation or sports manager. Companies have established that healthy employees are productive employees, and that employee fitness can significantly reduce an employer's cost for employee health care. Therefore, from a management standpoint, an understanding of workmen's compensation is equally as important as other liability concerns.

Workmen's compensation was born out of the harsh industrial age. Its beginnings were various rudimentary state and federal laws intended to provide minimum financial protection for workers and their families from maiming, disabling, or fatal industrial accidents. The purpose of workmen's compensation remains to simplify and reduce the financial uncertainty faced by employees who are injured on the job. Unlike other theories of liability, workmen's compensation is a no fault system. It is intended to eliminate, or at least minimize, potential tension in the employer-employee relationship arising from the injury.

Workmen's compensation facilitates the no fault basis through an exchange between the employer and the employee. An employee who suffers a job-related injury, sickness, or disease gives up his or her right to sue the employer for full damages in exchange for the speedy settlement and payment of medical costs, a portion of lost wages, and specified amount of compensation for temporary or permanent disabilities. The employer, in exchange for the quick settlement and payment of the approved claim, gives up the right to any legal defenses that he or she could have raised against the claim.

Today, in addition to industrial accidents, workmen's compensation recognizes the occupational hazards from stress, allergies, and job-related exposure to disease. Unfortunately, while the types of compensable employee injuries have been expanded, many of the legal tests initially applied to workmen's compensation have not kept the same pace. For example, during its early years, workmen's compensation only covered injuries resulting from "accidents." Many states continue to restrict workmen's compensation benefits to sickness, illness, or disease which results from an accidental cause. The burden of proof on the employee to connect his or her illness or disease to a specific job-related accident or event can be very difficult.

The compensation paid to the employee as a result of an injury is determined by schedules of payments approved by the state legislature. States usually have an administrative agency which processes and adjudicates employee claims. The administrative agency is the sole judge of whether an injury is job-related. The role of the courts is usually limited to insuring that an employer-employee relationship existed, and that the agency's decision regarding the job-relation was supported by sufficient evidence.

Obviously, there is a point of justifiable social and public policy to workmen's compensation. It serves an important labor interest by removing fault, and a potentially prolonged, adversarial process, from the employer-employee relationship. In order to serve that labor interest, workmen's compensation is an exclusive remedy; that is, an employee who suffers a job-related injury or illness can only recover medical costs and damages through workmen's compensation.[1] In *Swilley v. Sun Oil Company*, workmen's compensation was the only legal remedy available to an employee who lost the senses of taste and smell from an industrial accident. In *Ryherd v. Growmark, Inc.*, an employee who suffered lung damage from exposure to chemicals at his job site was limited to recovery through workmen's compensation for his disability.

The exclusive remedy for an employee's job-related injury is workmen's compensation, regardless if the injury is covered under its provisions.

SWILLEY V. SUN OIL COMPANY
506 So.2d 1364
Court of Appeal of Louisiana, 2nd Circuit
May 6, 1987

FACTS. An employee of Sun Oil Company inhaled a toxic substance while inspecting a gas cylinder. He suffered nerve damage to his face and head, resulting in the loss of taste and smell. Since the accident was job-related, the employee filed for workmen's compensation benefits. However, the court denied his claim because the Louisiana workmen's compensation law did not provide benefits for his type of permanent disability.

The employee then filed a tort action against the employer seeking recovery for the injury. However, his action was dismissed when the court ruled the employee was only eligible for benefits, if any, payable through workmen's compensation.

ISSUE. Workmen's compensation benefits are paid for medical costs, a portion of lost wages, and the temporary or permanent loss of use of some functions. In the present case, the employee sought benefits strictly for loss of use. His medical costs and one week term of disability were paid.

If an employee is injured in the scope of his employment, resulting in the loss of use of a function which is not covered under workmen's compensation, should the employee have the right to sue the employer in tort?

DECISION. Workmen's compensation is an exclusive remedy. If the loss of use of certain functions is not covered, and no benefits are payable, the employee is still precluded from any recovery through a tort action.

> "The plaintiff gave up his right to sue the employer in tort for the full extent of his damages. The employer accepted responsibility, without proof of fault on its part and without the benefit of affirmative defenses, for plaintiff's medical expenses and the payment of weekly benefits during the period of plaintiff's disability, if any. The fact that the disability in this case does not extend beyond one or two weeks does not diminish the value of the trade-off to the employee, the employer, or the public." (p. 1368)

Work-related injuries and diseases are covered by workmen's compensation unless intentionally caused by the employer.

RYHERD V. GROWMARK, INC.
509 N.E.2d 113
Appellate Court of Illinois, 4th District
June 2, 1987

FACTS. The plaintiff filed a lawsuit against his employer alleging that his supervisor fraudulently misrepresented the working conditions. The plaintiff suffered lung damage from exposure to various chemical substances during his employment. He alleged that he did not terminate his employment because a supervisor told him the chemicals were safe. His reliance on that statement led to the aggravation of his disease.

The court dismissed the suit, and ruled that the plaintiff's only remedy was workmen's compensation or the Occupational Diseases Act since his lung disease was from work-related causes.

ISSUE. Under Illinois law, a claimant may sue his employer for damages when: the injury was not accidental, the injury did not occur in the course of employment, the injury did not arise out of employment, or the injury was not compensable under the Workmen's Compensation or Workers' Occupational Disease Act.

DECISION. Since the initial injury to the plaintiffs lungs was work-related, his exclusive remedy was through Workmen's Compensation. The initial lung disease was incurred "in the line of duty," that is, it arose out of and in the course of employment. Illinois law does not provide a separate cause of action for aggravation of the injury or disease.

The plaintiff cited a California case which allowed a separate lawsuit for aggravation of an injury caused by an employer's intentional misconduct. The court distinguished that case, however, by noting that the employer's conduct in that instance went far beyond the concealment of dangerous exposure to chemicals.

JOB-RELATED INJURIES

A job-related injury is one which arises out of and occurs in the course of the employment. The injury must be established by proof of both elements. Therefore, an employee's injury which occurred in the course of the employment is not compensable unless it also arose out of the employment.[2] There are a number of other distinctive features to these general rules that we will examine throughout the chapter.

Arising Out Of and In the Course of the Employment

An injury arises out of the employment when it results from a risk or condition of employment. An injury does not arise out of the employment if it results from risks which are common to the general public. In that respect, it is more difficult for an employee to prove that an injury arose out of the employment than in the course of the employment. The primary difficulty is distinguishing risks which are truly unique to the job from common risks.[3] A means of determining the risk or condition factor of the employment is to ask: "except for the employment, would the employee have been injured?" For example, smoking on the job is a common risk, not a work-related risk (*Coleman v. Cycle Transformer Corporation*); allergies also are common risks unless their cause can be linked to a distinctive employment feature (*Chadwick v. Public Service Company of New Mexico* and *Farmers Rural Electric Cooperative v. Cooper*).

An injury caused by a smoking accident is not a compensable risk of employment for workmen's compensation.

COLEMAN V. CYCLE TRANSFORMER CORPORATION
520 A.2d 1341
Supreme Court of New Jersey
November 14, 1986

FACTS. An employee of Cycle Transformer Corporation was on lunch break in the lunchroom provided by the employer. The employer provided the dining area, tables, and chairs. Employees brought their own lunches, and were not paid for their lunch period. When the claimant finished her lunch, she lit a match for a cigarette, and caught her hair on fire.

Her claim for workmen's compensation benefits was denied by the court which ruled that her facial and head burns, scarring, and other disabilities did not arise out of her employment.

ISSUE. The workmen's compensation statute in New Jersey provided benefits for employees injured by accident arising out of and in the course of their employment. Was this injury a risk of the claimant's employment?

DECISION. It was easily determined that the injury occurred "in the course of employment," that is, at a time, place, and under circumstances in relation to her employment. Smoking on the job premises is customary and should reasonably be expected.

However, the injury did not "arise out of employment." It was not the result of a risk which might have been contemplated when she entered her employment, or as an incident to her employment:

"... an accident arises out of the employment when it is due to a condition of the employment." (p. 1346)

No condition of her employment caused the injury. The use of matches or smoking cigarettes was not a risk of her employment.

An allergy is not an occupational disease unless it is caused by the claimant's job, not the work place.

CHADWICK V. PUBLIC SERVICE COMPANY OF NEW MEXICO
731 P.2d 968
Court of Appeals of New Mexico
December 2, 1986

FACTS. The claimant was employed by the Public Service Company of New Mexico as a journeyman mechanical foreman at a generating station. He developed a rash diagnosed as contact dermatitis. It appeared to be caused by substances in the atmosphere at the generating plant. When he stopped working at the plant, the rash disappeared.

His claim for benefits under New Mexico's Occupational Disease Disablement Law was disallowed by the court which ruled that the allergy was not a compensable occupational disease.

ISSUE. The court defined the issue as:

"Whether (an allergy) is an occupational disease depends upon whether there is a recognizable link between the disease and some distinctive feature of the claimant's job." (p. 970)

DECISION. The allergy must be related to the claimant's *job*, not to a particular workplace. The court said: "...an ailment does not become an occupational disease simply because it is contracted on the employer's premises." (p. 970)

Since the allergy apparently resulted from the workplace, not from the claimant's work as a journeyman mechanical foreman, the allergy was not an occupational disease.

Employee's allergic reaction to computer terminals requires proof of a work-related cause for workmen's compensation benefits.

FARMERS RURAL ELECTRIC COOPERATIVE V. COOPER
715 S.W.2d 478
Court of Appeals of Kentucky
August 29, 1986

FACTS. A billing clerk with Farmers Rural Electric Cooperative starting exhibiting allergic symptoms when the Cooperative computerized its operations. She continued to suffer shortness of breath, sore throat, and numbness until she was transferred to another department with no computer terminals. Though the irritant could not specifically be identified, a number of physicians believed the symptoms resulted from exposure to the computer terminals.

She suffered no further symptoms until all of the offices of the Cooperative were computerized. She was forced to leave her employ when the allergy returned.

The court rejected her claim for workmen's compensation benefits ruling there was not substantial evidence to show the allergy was work-related.

ISSUE. Is the claimant required to identify an allergy irritant in order to claim workmen's compensation benefits?

DECISION. There was no question that the employee suffered an allergic reaction every time she was exposed to computer terminals. Therefore, the inability to identify the irritant alone would not justify dismissing her claim.

However, before that allergic condition can be considered a compensable injury under workmen's compensation, she had to prove a work-related injury, or a pre-existing condition aggravated by a work-related injury. Her burden of proof, the rule of "substantial evidence," required more than a showing that she became ill at work because of allergic reaction to an unidentified substance.

An injury which arises out of the employment usually occurs in the course of employment. Obviously, if a risk of the employment has caused the employee's injury, then it safely can be assumed that the injury occurred at a time, or at a place, or under a circumstance dictated by the employer. However, an injury which occurs in the course of employment may not arise out of the employment. That is, because an injury occurred during work, at the workplace, does not mean it resulted from a risk of employment.

The widow of an employee who was shot to death in the employee parking lot is awarded workmen's compensation death benefits.

BLAW-KNOX FOUNDRY & MILL MACHINERY, INC. V. DACUS
505 N.E.2d 101
Court of Appeals of Indiana
March 18, 1987

FACTS. The decedent, an employee of Blaw-Knox, was shot to death in the employee parking lot by an unknown assailant. He was in the employee parking lot late at night preparing to leave the premises from his afternoon shift. The parking lot was fenced and kept locked for the safety of employees, except during shift changes.

His wife's claim for workmen's compensation death benefits was granted over the appeal of the employer who argued that the employee's death was not the result of a risk or hazard incidental to his employment.

ISSUE. Benefits are awarded for injuries (or death) which arise out of and in the course of employment. The phrases "arise out of" and "in the course of" have separate meanings, and must be separately proven for a valid claim. Did decedent's death arise out of and in the course of his employment?

DECISION. "In the course of employment" refers to the time, place, and circumstance of the injury. When the injury occurs during the time, place, within the duties of employment, or during a reasonable period before or after work, it occurs in the course of employment.

"Arose out of employment" refers to the cause of injury. If there is a causal relationship between the employment and the injury, if there is a risk of injury resulting from the employment, or if it can be reasonably foreseen that the injury will occur as a result of the employment, then it arises out of the employment.

The decedent was shot to death in a lot which was usually closed due to its dangerous location. However, his work hours required his presence in the lot late at night, so that his risk of injury was greater than that to which members of the general public would be exposed. His death occurred at a time and place which was in the course of his employment, and was the result of a risk imposed by his employment; therefore, the injury arose out of his employment.

In its early years, workmen's compensation did not consider an employee's injury to be job-related unless it occurred on the employer's premises, during regular work hours, and from a specific job function for which the employee was paid. If those criteria were applied today, the benefits would not have been awarded in the *Blaw-Knox* case, since the decedent was not working at the time of his death.

However, gauging the time, place, and circumstance of an employee's injury is applied more liberally today. For example, the "reasonable time" rule could have been applied in the *Blaw-Knox* case. That rule provides that employees will be compensated for injuries occurring within a reasonable time of the start or the end of their work day, while they are still on the employer's premises.[4]

Causal Connection

"In the course of the employment," is a workmen's compensation concept measured by the time, location, and circumstance of an employee's injury. It directly relates, in varying degrees, to other factors such as work time or free time, paid duties or non-paid duties, and whether the injury occurred on or off the employer's premises.

The necessary causal connection between the job and an employee's injury is established when the injury "arises out of and in the course of employment." That test appears to have more restrictions placed on the time, place, and circumstance factors than on the risk or condition of employment element. However, the courts apply a broader interpretation of the "in the course of" element of the test. The courts remain more conservative in their approach to the risks of employment. For example, in the *Dade County School Board v. Polite* case, one of the issues was the "going to - coming from" work rule in workmen's compensation. Under that general rule, employees who are injured while in transit to and from work usually are denied workmen's compensation benefits. However, the general application of that rule creates many inequities; the courts are prone to be liberal in their application.

A physical education teacher's voluntary attendance at a track meet is within the course of her employment.

DADE COUNTY SCHOOL BOARD V. POLITE
495 So.2d 795
District Court of Appeal of Florida
September 18, 1986

FACTS. A full-time teacher in the Dade County (Florida) school system, taught physical education at North Glade Elementary School in the mornings, and at Lake Stevens Elementary School in the afternoons. On the day of her injury, she requested permission to leave Lake Stevens early to attend a track meet involving some of her students from North Glade. When permission was granted, she took some athletic equipment, intending to return it to Lake Stevens school after the meet.

She assisted with officiating and supervision at the track meet. While returning the equipment to the Lake Stevens after the meet, she was injured when her vehicle was struck by a hit-and-run driver.

She was granted workmen's compensation benefits over the appeal of the school board.

ISSUE. Workmen's compensation benefits are awarded for an injury which arises out of and in the course of the employment. However, there is a "going to or coming from" rule which excludes benefits for an employee who is injured either going to or coming from work. Was the teacher's injury work-related?

DECISION. The teacher was not required or paid to attend the track meet. However, after school participation was considered an important aspect in teacher performance evaluations. Therefore, she was in the course of her employment.

Although an employee going to or coming from work is not within the scope of employment, that exclusion does not totally preclude an award of benefits. In this instance, the court did not apply the going to or coming from rule because the teacher was performing her final duty of the day (returning the equipment) at the time of her accident.

Occupational Diseases

The recognition of job-related diseases by workmen's compensation has been slow for two reasons. First, workmen's compensation statutes in many states still require an accidental cause or a precipitating event for the employment-related injury. This type of restrictive application disregards diseases which are acquired over a period of time. Second, it is difficult to determine if a disease is job-related, or if it is one that equally threatens the general population. In *Grayson v.*

Gulf Oil Company, the inhalation of petrochemical odor from a co-worker triggered an allergic reaction that the court determined was a work-related, accidental injury.

A sudden, severe allergic reaction to chemicals is an accidental injury, not an occupational disease, in workmen's compensation.

GRAYSON V. GULF OIL COMPANY
357 S.E.2d 479
Court of Appeals of South Carolina
May 26, 1987

FACTS. The claimant worked for Gulf Oil Company since 1965. In the course of her employ through 1984, she was exposed to large quantities of gasoline. In 1982, when her employer suffered evaportation of large amounts of gasoline due to storage tank problems, the claimant began experiencing severe allergic symptoms of chemical insensitivity to gasoline. The cumulative effects began manifesting themselves in late 1983. In 1984, the reactions became so severe that the claimant had to leave her employ. It was her doctor's opinion that the constant exposure to petrochemicals had affected her immune system so that she suffered an allergic "cascade" to her environment during the last few months of her employment.

The court awarded her workmen's compensation benefits ruling that her dysfunction was the result of aggravation of a pre-existing disease arising out of and in the course of her employ.

ISSUE. Was the allergic reaction a compensable "accident?"

DECISION. The court determined that this particular dysfunction was the result of an accident, that is, a condition by chance or without design, occurring unexpectedly or unintentionally.

The 19-year exposure to chemicals led to the first reaction in October, 1983; rapid deterioration of her condition; then complete collapse of her immune system in 1984. The court cited:

> "Where a sudden illness or collapse is precipitated by the inhalation of harmful elements at a definite time, which brings to a climax the cumulative deleterious effects of the inhalation of such elements in the course of the employment over a period of time, it is generally considered that the disability is attributable to an accidental injury rather than an occupational disease." 82 Am. Jur.2d *Workmen's Compensation*, Sec. 303 (1976)

Occupational diseases are difficult to establish. A disease caused by exposure to elements at the work place may be affected by exposure to non-work elements as well. Therefore, many states modify application of the "in the course of and arise out of" test to a comparison rule. If the work place exposes an employee to a disease, the courts will concentrate on whether the risk created by the exposure is greater for the employee as a result of the employment than it would be for a member of the general public. There are a number of theories which deal with employment-related exposure. The following cases tested job-related exposure to specific diseases. In *Duckett v. Alaska Steel Co.*, a smoker who developed lung disease alleged the disease was caused by his work-related exposure to asbestos fibers; in *Collins v. Mills*, another smoker argued that his obstructive lung disease resulted from job-related exposure to cotton dust; and in *Gachioch v. Stroh Brewery Company*, an alcoholic claimed his alcoholism resulted from Stroh's free beer policy for its workers.

Smoking, rather than work-related exposure to asbestos fibers, was determined to be the cause of a lung cancer.

DUCKETT V. ALASKA STEEL CO.
735 P.2d 1289
Court of Appeals of Oregon
April 22, 1987

FACTS. The claimant worked for Alaska Steel Co. and Scrap Processors from 1960 until 1979. During the time of his employ, he was constantly exposed to asbestos fibers. In 1980, his left lung was removed as a result of a lung carcinoma. His workmen's compensation claim for occupational disease benefits was denied when the hearing referee determined that a 30-year, two-three packs-per-day smoking habit was the cause of the carcinoma.

ISSUE. What evidence supported the determination that smoking rather than exposure to asbestos caused the cancer?

DECISION. The claimant's case was based on his exposure to above-normal levels of asbestos during his employment. He also relied on the fact that a lung specialist incorrectly located the carcinoma. The specialist testified the location of the carcinoma was centrally located in the lung, indicating a smoking cause; in fact, the surgery revealed the tumor was located in the lower left portion, suggesting a different cause.

However, four physicians testified that smoking was the most likely cause of the disease. Further, there were no fibrosis, plaques, or thickening present in the claimant's lungs. This was persuasive that the carcinoma was caused by the smoking, not asbestos.

Obstructive lung disease is an occupational disease only if it developed as a result of exposure to work-related causes.

COLLINS V. MILLS
354 S.E.2d 245
Court of Appeals of North Carolina
April 7, 1987

FACTS. A 36-year employee of Cone Mills (North Carolina), performed a number of duties that exposed him to cotton dust. He also smoked a pack of cigarettes a day for most of his working career.

Following his retirement, he filed a claim for workmen's compensation when he discovered that he had obstructive lung disease. His claim for workmen's compensation benefits was denied by the North Carolina Industrial Commission which ruled that the obstructive lung disease had been caused by smoking, not cotton dust.

ISSUE. How did the court determine the disease was caused by smoking?

DECISION. A disease is considered an occupational disease if the occupation exposes the employee to a greater chance of contracting the disease than the general public, and if the exposure significantly contributes to, or causes, the development of the disease.

The medical evidence established that the obstructive lung disease was caused by the cigarette smoking, not the exposure to cotton dust. The evidence concluded that the claimant would have suffered from the lung disease even if he had never worked in the mill. The exposure to cotton dust, therefore, had not been a significant factor to the development of the disease.

Workmen's compensation benefits will not be awarded for chronic alcoholism.

GACHIOCH V. STROH BREWERY COMPANY
396 N.W.2d 1
Supreme Court of Michigan
November 25, 1986

FACTS. The claimant worked at Stroh Brewery since 1947. At the time of his employ, he had control of his alcoholic tendencies. As part of its union agreement, Stroh's provided unlimited free beer to employees during lunch and rest breaks.

The claimant, who worked on the production line, increased his consumption of beer over the years to 9-12 bottles per day. By 1973, he had developed a severe drinking problem. He made an agreement with Stroh's to quit drinking beer on the job. He broke that agreement. He entered into another non-drinking agreement which he also violated. He was fired in 1974 for intoxication on the job.

He was granted workmen's compensation benefits for his alcoholism as an occupational disability. The Michigan Supreme Court, however, reversed the award, ruling the Workmen's Compensation Appeals Board did not apply the correct legal test for occupational diseases.

ISSUE. What is the legal test for determining whether a disease is an occupational disease or an ordinary disease?

DECISION. The standard to determine whether or not the disease is compensable or not is:

> "Personal Injury shall include a disease or disability which is due to cause and conditions which are characteristic of and peculiar to the business of the employer and which arises out of and in the course of employment. Ordinary diseases of life to which the public is generally exposed outside of the employment shall not be compensable." (p. 3)

Workmen's compensation benefits for an occupational disease would be granted if the disease was from causes or conditions which are inherent to the business of Stroh Brewery, and which arose out of and in the course of employment. The claimant had to prove that his alcoholism was due to a characteristic of his work duties at Stroh's. Alcoholism was a general disease to which the claimant was also exposed outside the confines of his employment.

Occupational diseases do not lend themselves to easy legal definition. The courts search for a causal factor between the employment and the disease; the measure of that causal factor is whether the employment "significantly" contributed to the disease.

PROBLEMS WITH STRESS

Stress, similar to occupational diseases, has only recently been recognized as a compensable feature in workmen's compensation. That recognition is limited by the courts' frustrations with the variable degrees of causal connection between employment-related stress and the employee's injury. How does stress fit within the "arise out of and in the course of" test? Some courts have examined stress as a risk or condition of the employment. In *Reid v. Gamb, Inc.* and *Talley v. Enserch Corporation*, the courts concentrated on whether the stress was extraordinary, or much greater than would be usually experienced in a non-work setting.

A stroke must be caused by extraordinary work-related mental or emotional stress to be a compensable injury under workmen's compensation.

REID V. GAMB, INC.
499 So.2d 644
Court of Appeal of Louisiana, 3rd Circuit
December 10, 1986

FACTS. The claimant was the district manager for five restaurants owned by the defendant. He was resting in a motel in another town when he suffered a stroke. He had just completed an exhausting day preparing for the opening of a new restaurant.

His claim for workmen's compensation benefits was denied when the court ruled that his stroke did not "arise out of his employment."

ISSUE. If job-related mental or emotional stress caused the stroke, should the claimant be eligible for workmen's compensation benefits?

DECISION. The court concluded that the stroke occurred while the claimant was "in the course of his employment"; that is, he was engaged in his employer's business, and that business required him to be at the motel at the time of the stroke.

However, for an injury to be compensable, it must also "arise out of the employment," be caused by work-related risks. The claimant failed to prove that the stroke was caused by extraordinary, work-related mental or emotional stress. The evidence regarding the stress of his job did not indicate any worry, nervousness, over-work, or any disagreements or accidents.

Although it was clear the claimant worked long hours and did a great deal of traveling, the medical evidence concluded that a great deal more stress would be required to cause or contribute to a stroke.

A heart attack suffered on the golf course is found to be job-related under Louisiana workmen's compensation.

TALLEY V. ENSERCH CORPORATION
508 So.2d 197
Court of Appeal of Louisiana, 3rd Circuit
May 13, 1987

FACTS. The claimant was a divisional manager for Enserch Corporation. He was charged with the task of setting up a new oil operation in Oklahoma. He commuted on a regular basis between Oklahoma and Louisiana, where his family resided. Due to manpower shortage, he had to assume some physical duties in addition to his supervisory role. Four days before his first heart attack, he was up all night loading pipe for a job site.

The first heart attack occurred on the golf course while the claimant was playing with another company officer and a business acquaintance. A second heart attack occurred approximately two weeks later after claimant had returned to Louisiana to recuperate with his family. Following the second attack, he underwent by-pass surgery, and never returned to his employment.

The employer disputed his claim for workmen's compensation, in part, alleging that the heart attack did not arise out of or occur in the course of employment. The court disagreed and ruled that it was a work-related injury.

ISSUE. Is a heart attack suffered on a golf course a compensable injury under workmen's compensation?

DECISION. The court ruled that part of the claimant's duties required that he entertain customers and business acquaintances; golf was an acceptable means of doing business. In fact, all of the claimant's golf fees, including golf balls, were paid by his employer who encouraged that recreational activity for its business benefit. Thus, the injury was suffered in the course of employment.

The court further ruled that setting up the new operation in a declining oil market, the manpower shortage, and his separation from family were stress and strain much greater than might be experienced in a non-work situation. Thus, the injury arose out of the employment, and was compensable.

Job-Related Stress

Establishing a causal connection between job-related stress and a resulting employee injury requires some insight into job motivation. For instance, in *Ryan v. Connor*, the court recognized that an employee's anticipation of a forced retirement could be a work-related stress. However, in *McVey v. General Motors Corporation*, an employee's anxiety and stress about his job performance and abilities was not a work-related cause of a heart condition. The fear of job loss and its consequences can produce work-related stresses, as in *Jones v. District of Columbia Department of Employment Services* and *Mayeux v. Weiser Security Services, Inc.*

The stress of a forced retirement may be a work-related cause of a compensable death under workmen's compensation.

RYAN V. CONNOR
503 N.E.2d 1379
Supreme Court of Ohio
December 30, 1986

FACTS. A 45-year employee of the J. B. Foote Foundry, was informed that the company wanted him to take early retirement. The employee experienced stress, agitation, trembling, and other symptoms after two meetings with company management. The day after the last meeting with the company, he suffered a fatal heart attack while trimming the trees around his home.

Prior to his death, Ohio did not recognize disabilities solely caused by emotional stress as compensable injuries under workmen's compensation. Thus, the Industrial Commission denied the widow's claim for workmen's compensation death benefits.

However, on appeal, the Ohio Supreme Court overruled its previous decisions, and stated that injuries caused solely by stress arising out of and in the course of employment were compensable injuries. The case was sent back for a new trial.

ISSUE. What standards did the Ohio Supreme Court establish for determining whether stress-related injuries were compensable under workmen's compensation?

DECISION. Despite strong dissent by some members of the court, the majority of the court viewed their decision as "joining the mainstream of American jurisprudence."

It adopted the test of the New York Court of Appeals which held that the claimant had to prove the injury resulted from a greater emotional strain than that to which all other employees were occasionally subjected. Further, there must be a direct causal relationship between the stress and the disability.

Heart disease must be related to specific events or stress at work to be a compensable injury under workmen's compensation.

McVEY V. GENERAL MOTORS CORPORATION, FISHER BODY
DIVISION
408 N.W.2d 408
Court of Appeals of Michigan
March 27, 1987

FACTS. The claimant worked for General Motors for 24 years, part of which was an extremely stressful position in the assembly line control room. When he left that duty and returned to electrical construction, he became depressed that he was not as educated or knowledgeable as the younger electricians. He began experiencing chest pains, nausea, and other heart disease symptoms. It was determined that he suffered from arteriosclerosis with angina, and an "anxiety state."

The court rejected his workmen's compensation claim for total disability based on work-related stress because he failed to establish a causal connection between the heart damage and his work.

ISSUE. The claimant offered the testimony of a physician who firmly established the medical problem, and a psychiatrist who rendered an opinion that the claimant's return to work would produce stress which would ultimately induce a heart attack. Why did the court reject his claim?

DECISION. The evidence disclosed that the claimant had smoked a pack of cigarettes per day for nearly 50 years, suffered from ulcers and a previous stroke, and was more than was 66-years-old.

The claimant failed to establish a relationship between the heart damage and specific causes at work. His only evidence consisted of general allegations of stress and anxiety over the period of his employ. He was unable to show any precipitating events or incidents likely to cause his heart condition. The fact that he experienced chest pains was not sufficient to establish his claim.

There was no evidence that his nervous condition prohibited him from carrying out his assigned duties. His state of mind was found to be a result of a heart condition which was not work- related.

Is a heart attack caused by the stress of impending job loss a compensable injury under workmen's compensation?

JONES V. DISTRICT OF COLUMBIA DEPARTMENT OF EMPLOYMENT SERVICES
519 A.2d 704
District of Columbia Court of Appeals
January 14, 1987

FACTS. A 35-year employee of the Potomac Electric Power Company (PEPCO) was caught drinking on the job. He was given a five-day suspension pending a hearing to determine whether he should be permanently discharged. During the suspension period, his behavior changed dramatically. He grew irritable and angry, and suffered withdrawal and vomiting. The day before the discharge hearing, he unexpectedly died of a heart attack.

His wife's claim for workmen's compensation death benefits was denied when the Department of Employment Services (DOES) ruled that his death was not an "accidental" injury, and that as a matter of public policy, there should be no recovery for injuries caused by emotional distress attributable to disciplinary actions.

The District of Columbia Court of Appeals reversed that decision because the DOES failed to consider whether job-related stress caused the heart attack.

ISSUE. The three elements for a compensable injury under District of Columbia law were: (1) the injury must be an accidental, (2) it must arise out employment, and (3) it must be in the course of employment. Therefore, was the heart attack caused by job-related stress?

DECISION. The court stated:

> " . . . the question whether a claim presents a compensable 'accidental injury' does not depend on whether the employment event which allegedly caused it was an emotional or a physical stressor, or whether that stressor was usual or unusual. Rather, the injury, to be 'accidental,' need only be something that unexpectedly goes wrong within the human frame. A heart attack clearly can meet that test." (p. 709)

The DOES determined that the disciplinary action was not an unusual employment event, thus, the resulting injury was not an accidental injury. However, the agency failed to address the other two elements for compensable injury, specifically, whether or not the injury was caused by or related to the job.

A heart attack must be caused by work-related stress or exertion to be compensable under Louisiana workmen's compensation.

MAYEUX V. WEISER SECURITY SERVICES, INC.
508 So.2d 132
Court of Appeal of Louisiana, 4th Circuit
May 12, 1987

FACTS. The decedent, who was recovering from a heart attack, returned to work without medical authorization. He was concerned about his family's finances; he accepted a job as a night security guard at a motel.

On the night of his death, he spoke to the desk clerk before starting his rounds. Approximately five minutes later, he returned and told the clerk to call an ambulance because he was suffering another heart attack. He spoke with the doctors and his wife prior to his death, but did not mention any problems prior to the attack.

His family's claim for workmen's compensation burial and death benefits was denied because they failed to prove that work-related stress or exertion preceded the heart attack.

ISSUE. A compensable accident in the state of Louisiana must arise out of and occur during the course of employment. There is no question that the heart attack occurred in the course of employment. How did the court conclude that the heart attack did not arise out of the employment?

DECISION. The evidence disclosed the decedent suffered his first heart attack as a result of high blood pressure, hypertension, and nervousness. However, during the year since his first heart attack, he never quit his two packs-per-day smoking habit, nor did he adhere to his special diet.

While his concern over his family's financial plight led him back to work without medical authorization, it was impossible to determine what precipitated the heart attack. The court said, "They (the doctors) said a number of factors, including caffeine consumption, cigarette smoking, stress from financial problems, arteriosclerosis, etc., could have caused the death." (p. 135)

The court further stated:

> "For the heart attack to arise out of or be connected with the employment, the exertion, stress or strain, acting upon the pre-existing disease, must be of a degree greater than that generated in everyday non-employment life." (p. 134)

The opposing decisions of *Ryan* and *McVey* illustrate the difficulty the courts have relating stress to work-related injuries. There is no question that an employee's concern over job skills and expertise are legitimate concerns; and, it should be expected that those fears might contribute to a stress-induced illness. But, those are stresses which are shared by all workers in the free enterprise system. Therefore, the courts do not distinguish those stresses as job-related causes.

Because workmen's compensation laws are based on the "accidental" injury concept, the courts scrutinize for any precipitating events prior to the injury.[5] That examination has impacted on two areas: stress as a cause of job-related injuries, and the effect of stress on pre-existing conditions.

Stress and Heart Injuries

Many times employees are suffering from a medical condition at the time of their employ. In those cases, the employers take the employees as "they find them." An employee who suffers from a pre-existing medical condition at the time of his hire, is not automatically precluded from coverage. If the employment significantly contributes to the deterioration of that condition, the employee is eligible for workmen's compensation benefits.

Significant contribution is difficult to prove. The courts are likely to rely on an accidental or precipitating event for the causal connection. This is most vividly portrayed in heart attack cases such as *State Industrial Insurance System v. Weaver*, where a mile-run was the precipitating cause of a fatal heart attack; and *McDonough v. Connecticut Bank and Trust Company*, when job criticism precipitated severe chest pains.

Workmen's compensation death benefits are awarded to the widow of an employee who suffered a fatal heart attack within minutes of completing a timed mile-run.

STATE INDUSTRIAL INSURANCE SYSTEM V. WEAVER
734 P.2d 740
Supreme Court of Nevada
March 31, 1987

FACTS. A 59-year-old security inspector for the Department of Energy collapsed and died within minutes of completing a timed mile run required for his job retention. The decedent had been examined and cleared to participate in the mile run, though the autopsy disclosed he suffered from coronary disease.

His widow's claim for death benefits under the Nevada Industrial Insurance Act was allowed by court.

ISSUE. Nevada law provides that death benefits are awarded if the employee's cause of death is an injury by accident arising out of and in the course of employment.

DECISION. Heart attacks caused by sudden, unforeseen, and violent application of force, and precipitated by job-related events are compensable injuries. The court adopted the rule of the Colorado Supreme Court: when death occurs within a short time after a blow or overexertion in the course of employment, a presumption arises that the death was caused by the employment, and the claimant is not required to establish causation by expert medical testimony.

The court found a clear causal relationship between the required mile run and the fatal heart attack. The victim, despite his age, was subjected to the extraordinary and violent physical stress of a mile run in the Nevada desert. While his job duties over a 17-year career had not required running, he was required to complete the mile run within a specified time in order to retain his job. The immediate physical response to the run was evidence of a violent causative force.

A sudden change in physical condition is proof of accidental injury for workmen's compensation.

McDONOUGH V. CONNECTICUT BANK AND TRUST COMPANY
527 A.2d 664
Supreme Court of Connecticut
June 16, 1987

FACTS. The claimant was a 58-year-old female who had a family history of heart disease, had an extensive cigarette smoking habit, and was overweight. She worked for her employer for 21 years, the last three in a supervisory capacity. During a meeting when work problems were being discussed, some criticism was leveled at the claimant. She left the meeting in tears. Two days later she received a memo detailing aspects of the meeting with which she did not agree. Following another meeting, she became upset and went home where she began experiencing severe chest pains. Over the course of the next year, the claimant was treated for disabling heart disease.

The court granted her claim for workmen's compensation benefits, finding that the heart disease was caused by work-related stress.

ISSUE. Her employer disputed the cause of the heart problems alleging there was no distinct physical injury, such as death of a portion of heart tissue, and that the cause of the heart disease may have been caused by non-employment factors as easily as employment factors.

DECISION. The court affirmed that an injury is compensable if work-related mental or nervous stress has caused the injury. However, it rejected the contention that a precise physical injury had to be shown.

The court further ruled that a sudden, unusual, and unexpected change in physical condition is sufficient to prove an accidental injury. The proof of a direct causal connection between the injury, whether disease or accident, and the employment itself, is sufficient to establish causation.

In *Wiggs Construction v. Knowles*, a claimant who suffered a heart attack as the result of extraordinary job-related exertion was protected by workmen's compensation.

A heart attack caused by exertion not routine to the job of a carpenter is a compensable injury under workmen's compensation.

WIGGS CONSTRUCTION V. KNOWLES
497 So.2d 942
District Court of Appeal of Florida, 1st District
November 13, 1986

FACTS. The claimant was a 58-year-old carpenter who had worked for Wiggs Construction Company for 30 years. His general duties were supervisory and light trim work. However, on the day of his injury (a hot and humid day), he was lifting 4' x 8' plywood sections by himself (a job that normally required two men). He suffered a heart attack after three and a one-half hours of this type of work.

His claim for workmen's compensation was granted. The court denied the employer's appeal that he failed to prove the heart attack had been caused by non-routine work activities.

ISSUE. The court said:

"A determination of the compensability of a heart attack caused by unusual strain or overexertion is 'not . . . predicated on the broad question of what was routine to the claimant; rather, that inquiry must necessarily be circumscribed by a consideration of what was routine to the job the claimant was accustomed to performing,' at the time of the claim." (p. 944)

DECISION. The excessive heat and humidity, combined with the lifting of the plywood sheets, was an exertion not routine to the general carpentry work for which he had been hired. On that basis, the heart attack was a compensable injury.

Stress and exertion are synonymous terms concerning heart-related injuries. Although exertion connotes a physical movement, the courts recognize the physical attributes of stress as well.

The exact time of a heart attack does not have to be determined to be a compensable injury under workmen's compensation.

SOUTHWIRE COMPANY V. EASON
353 S.E.2d 567
Court of Appeals of Georgia
January 26, 1987

FACTS. An overweight female employee of Southwire Company, who also had a heavy smoking habit, suffered from heart disease. In addition, she came from a family with a history of coronary disease. During the summer months, she experienced chest pains when working in a hot and stuffy area. One day, she had severe chest pains that continued after she went home. An hour and a half after she had left work, the pain became so intense that she was unable to move.

She was awarded workmen's compensation benefits although only one of four physicians stated that her heart disease was work-related. None of the doctors could establish the exact time she suffered the small heart attack.

ISSUE. Georgia Workmen's Compensation law provides, in part:

> "heart disease, heart attack, the failure or occlusion of any of the coronary blood vessels, or thrombosis . . . must be shown by a preponderance of competent and credible evidence . . .to be attributable to the performance of the usual work of employment." (p. 568)

Why is this a compensable injury if the exact time of the heart attack cannot be determined?

DECISION. The court awarded workmen's compensation benefits on the following basis: first, the severe pain occurred within one and a half hours after she left work, and the medical testimony did show that physical or emotional stress could precipitate that type of pain as long as one hour after she left work; second, her work was physically and emotionally stressful; and, finally, her heart condition was aggravated by her employment.

Measuring extraordinary exertion or stress, however, has become a difficult task. The courts have formulated rules regarding exertion (physical or mental) based on whether the employee suffers from a pre-existing condition. If, for example, an employee without a history of heart problems suffered a heart attack, generally the employee would be covered by workmen's compensation if there was an ordinary, job-related exertion as a precipitating cause. If the employee had suffered from a pre-existing heart condition, then the court would look for an unusual, or extraordinary stress or exertion as the precipitating cause. In *Acoff v. General Motors Corporation,* the court denied benefits for a heart attack victim because there was no proof that work-related events precipitated the attack. In *Price River Coal Co. v. Industrial Commission of Utah*, the court sent the case back for a new trial to determine if the decedent, who suffered from heart disease, had died as the result of unusual or extraordinary work-related stress or exertion.

Heart damage must be related to specific incidents or events at work to be a compensable injury under Michigan Workmen's Compensation.

ACOFF V. GENERAL MOTORS CORPORATION
400 N.W.2d 95
Court of Appeals of Michigan
August 11, 1986

FACTS. The claimant inspected 12-14 pound castings, for General Motors, and packed them individually in containers. One day during a system backup, he began to experience pain in his legs, back, and left armpit. A couple of days later, he experienced severe pain which spread to the left side of his chest. He was hospitalized with an apparent heart attack.

The Workmen's Compensation Appeals Board (WCAB) granted his claim for workmen's compensation benefits finding that his disability was caused or aggravated by his employment. However, the court reversed the WCAB decision, and ruled that he had not established heart damage, or proved that incidents or events at work caused the disability.

ISSUE. Michigan Workmen's Compensation Law provides:

"Ordinary diseases of life to which the public is generally exposed outside of the employment shall not be compensable." (p. 96)

What was the claimant's burden of proof?

DECISION. He had to prove that there was heart damage, and that there was a connection or relationship between the heart damage and specific incidents or events at work. The court found that:

"General conclusions of stress, anxiety, and exertion over a period of time do not satisfy this second requirement." (p. 96)

The doctors did not establish that he had, in fact, suffered a heart attack. Therefore, he was unable to prove heart damage. Further, the court considered the WCAB finding too general to establish a legal connection between the claimed heart attack and specific incidents at work. The court stated: ". . .the mere occurrence of symptomatology while working, absent specific precipitating events at work, was insufficient to support a finding of compensability." (p. 97)

A heart attack must result from unusual exertion related to work activities to be a compensable injury under workmen's compensation.

PRICE RIVER COAL CO. V. INDUSTRIAL COMMISSION OF
UTAH
731 P.2d 1079
Supreme Court of Utah
December 31, 1986

FACTS. A miner, employed by the Price River Coal Co., was found dead of a heart attack in a mine. The miner, who suffered extensive heart disease, maintained underground conveyor belts in the normal course of the mine's operation. He was working alone on the day he died. There was conflicting evidence regarding what labor activities he was performing at the time of his death.

His widow was awarded workmen's compensation death benefits by the Industrial Commission. However, on appeal by the employer, the court reversed that award and sent the case back for new trial to establish what work-related activities he was performing at the time of death.

ISSUE. Utah awards workmen's compensation benefits to: "the dependents of every such employee who is killed, by accident arising out of or in the course of his employment." Is the miner's widow entitled to benefits?

DECISION. There was no question the miner's death was an accident based on the definition of "accident" adopted by the court: "Where either the cause of the injury or the result of an exertion was different from what would normally be expected to occur, the occurrence was unplanned, unforeseen, unintended and therefore 'by accident'." The miner's heart attack was unexpected and unintended, thus, an accident.

Since his death was an accident, it was necessary to determine whether it arose out of or in the course of employment. Causation is established when there is usual or ordinary exertion in the employment activity. However, if the employee suffers a pre-existing condition, then the employment activity must involve some unusual or extraordinary exertion exceeding the usual wear and tear, or exertions of non-employment life.

Since there was a pre-existing condition, the court sent the case back for a new trial to determine if there was extraordinary or unusual employment activity when he died.

Mental stress or exertion can be the cause of a work-related heart injury, as in *Boeing Vertol Company v. Workmen's Compensation Appeal Board (Coles).*

A physical injury caused by the psychological stresses of employment is compensable under workmen's compensation.

BOEING VERTOL COMPANY V. WORKMEN'S COMPENSA-
TION APPEAL BOARD (COLES)
528 A.2d 1020
Commonwealth Court of Pennsylvania
July 15, 1987

FACTS. An engineering writer, under great stress from his employer to produce a manual for a product being developed, suffered aggravation of a pre-existing cardiovascular disease. The evidence disclosed that when the writer was assigned the project, it was already behind schedule. Also, there were a number of meetings, discussions, and deadlines which left the claimant ill. A physician testified that the cardiovascular disease had been so aggravated that the engineer was unable to return to work for the employer, or to perform any type of work where he would be subject to anxiety, apprehension, or tension.

The claimant was awarded workmen's compensation benefits. The court affirmed the ruling of the hearing examiner that the aggravation of the disease was caused by stressful employment situations.

ISSUE. An employee who suffers a psychological injury resulting from a subjective reaction to normal work conditions is not eligible for workmen's compensation. Therefore, why did the court grant benefits for this injury?

DECISION. The court distinguished three types of mental or psychological categories of workmen's compensation cases:

1. psychological stimulus causing physical injury;

2. physical injury causing psychic injury; and

3. psychological injury causing psychic injury.

The employer attempted to equate the circumstances in this case to the third category. However, the court rejected that argument since the resulting injury was a physical disability. Under that circumstance, the court ruled the factual basis for awarding workmen's compensation for a *physical* injury was supported by substantial, competent, and credible evidence.

RECREATIONAL ACTIVITIES

With the increased awareness of employee mental/physical wellness and its apparent positive effect on job production and efficiency, it is necessary to examine employer-sponsored physical and recreational activities.

Recreational activities are distinguished by their intended results. Usually, a physical or recreational activity will benefit the employees' mental or physical health, and many times should improve employee morale and efficiency. However, those purposes alone are not sufficient to render a job-related recreational injury compensable under workmen's compensation. Conversely, an activity *required* by the employer would, more than likely, have a purpose other than improved employee morale. In that case, the resulting injury would be compensable since the activity primarily benefitted the employer.[6]

The first approach taken by the courts is a determination whether the injury occurred on the employer's premises. For example, if an employer has basketball or softball facilities for employee use during lunch, rest breaks, or non-work hours, a resulting injury from that use is usually compensable. However, some courts will disregard that presumption if no other benefit can be shown other than improved morale.

The majority of cases involving recreational injuries occur, however, off the employer's premises. In those cases, the court's presumption favors the employer. There is a heavy burden of proof required of the employee in a recreation injury claim.

A McDonald's employee is not eligible for workmen's compensation benefits for an injury suffered on the way to a softball game.

BLACK V. McDONALD'S OF LAYTON
733 P.2d 154
Supreme Court of Utah
February 6, 1987

FACTS. An employee of McDonald's in Layton, Utah, was injured in a car accident on his way to play a softball game. He played in a league established only for McDonald's employees. The various McDonald's restaurants in the area each donated $30 for trophies, balls, and scorebooks. The games were played during off-hours, there was no participation by the McDonald's Corporation, the team shirts did not contain McDonald's advertising or logos, and the stated purpose of the league was only to create better feelings among McDonald's employees.

The employee's claim for workmen's compensation benefits was denied because his injury did not arise out of or in the course of his employment.

ISSUE. What are the criteria for determining if a recreational injury is compensable under workmen's compensation?

DECISION. In Utah, the factors for determining a compensable recreational injury are:

1. time and place: games scheduled during working hours on the employer's premises are generally work-related; time and place can be decisive for determining compensable recreational injuries;

2. the degree of employer initiative, promotion, and sponsorship;

3. the financial support and equipment furnished by the employer; and

4. the degree of employer benefit, although improved work efficiency and morale alone are not enough to make the activity work-related.

The court determined that the injury was not compensable because the games were off the employer's premises, were conducted during off hours, and the employer's financial support was negligible.

The employer must receive a benefit more substantial than a tax deduction from the activity, as in *Wilson v. Scientific Software- Intercomp.*

The tax deduction for an employee ski trip must substantially benefit the employer in order to impose workmen's compensation liability.

WILSON V. SCIENTIFIC SOFTWARE-INTERCOMP
738 P.2d 400
Colorado Court of Appeals
February 5, 1987

FACTS. The claimant worked as an accounting clerk. His employer organized an employee ski trip and provided transportation and refreshments. Employees provided their own equipment, and paid their other fees and expenses. Participation was strictly voluntary, and the trip was held on a non-work day.

The claimant filed for workmen's compensation after he was injured in a skiing accident. The court rejected the claim ruling the only benefit of the trip to the employer was improved employee morale. Therefore, the accident did not arise out of and in the course of the claimant's employment.

ISSUE. When participation in a recreational event is voluntary and the only benefit to the employer is improved employee morale, an injury occurring from the activity is not compensable under workmen's compensation.

The claimant argued the ruling because the employer received a pecuniary benefit since the trip was tax deductible, and because he discussed business affecting the employer during the trip.

DECISION. The court ruled that there was no evidence that the pecuniary benefit of the tax deduction resulted in a net gain equal to or in excess of the amount expended for the trip. Thus, the court could not conclude there was a substantial benefit to the employer.

The business discussed by the employee was solely motivated by his own personal interest. There was no evidence that the employer gained any benefit from the discussions.

Further, the employer must be heavily involved in the specific activity, such as providing money, materials, work time and personnel. Intangibles, such as business promotion, must be specifically proven (*Law Offices of William W. Schooley v. Industrial Commission of Illinois*).

The Illinois Workmen's Compensation Act provides, in part:
"Accidental injuries incurred while participating in voluntary recreational programs including but not limited to athletic events, parties and picnics do not arise out of and in the course of employment even though the employer pays some or all the cost thereof. This exclusion shall not apply in the event that the injured employee was ordered or assigned by his employer to participate in the program." (p. 1188)

LAW OFFICES OF WILLIAM W. SCHOOLEY V. INDUSTRIAL
COMM. OF ILLINOIS
503 N.E.2d 1186
Appellate Court of Illinois, 5th District
February 3, 1987

FACTS. A law clerk, employed by his father's law firm, managed and played for a softball team co-sponsored by the firm and a local tavern. He injured his back in a game. His claim for workmen's compensation was originally denied by the Industrial Commission based on the above statute. However, the court reversed the decision, and awarded him workmen's compensation benefits.

ISSUE. When does a recreational activity injury arise out of and in the course of employment?

DECISION. The criteria for determining when a recreational activity arises out of and in the course of employment are: the extent of employer benefits, the extent of an employer's active organization, and the extent of employer sponsorship and required attendance.

The court found that the son was the team manager and player because of his father's involvement, that the firm paid for the team's beer at the tavern after the games, and that the team would not have been sponsored by the firm if not for the son's involvement. The evidence further disclosed the son was given time off from work for team activities (without loss of pay), that he used law office materials and supplies for team activities, and that the firm did get some business from team members or other acquaintances with the softball team.

REFERENCES

Darlington, L. and T.J. Knieser. 1980. *The Law and Economics of Workers' Compensation.* The Rand Institute for Civil Justice.

Hood, J.B. and B. Hardy. 1984. *Workers' Compensation and Employee Protection Laws.* Nutshell Series 1-84 St. Paul, MN: West Publishing Co.

Larson, A. 1985. *Workmen's Compensation for Occupational Injuries and Death.* Vol. I, Desk Ed. New York, NY: Matthew Bender and Company.

Malone, W., M. Plant, and J. Little. 1974. *The Employment Relation, Cases and Materials.* St. Paul, MN: West Publishing Co.

Workmen's Compensation for Recreational Activities. 1956.23 U. Chi. L. Rev. 328

Workmen's Compensation: The Personal Comfort Doctrine. 1960. Wis. L. Rev. 91

[1] There are a number of job-related injury situations where workmen's compensation is not the sole remedy. For example, the law recognizes the right of an employee to sue a co-employee in tort law if the co-employee negligently caused the injury outside the scope of his work duties. Generally, independent contractors are not considered employees for workmen's compensation purposes. The exclusive remedy concept only relates to injuries or diseases where the existence of an employer-employee relationship is not in issue.

[2] A notable exception to the "and" requirement is Utah's Workmen's Compensation statute which defines a compensable injury as: ". . .by accident arising out of *or* in the course of employment." *Compensation for Industrial Accidents to be Paid,* 4B Utah Code Annot., Section 35-1-45.

[3] Allergies are a separate illness for workmen's compensation purposes. The *Chadwick* case and the *Farmers Rural* case are included to highlight the differences between the time, place, and circumstance factor from the risk factors of employment.

[4] The Personal Comfort rule recognizes the need of employees to attend to their personal ministerations during the work day. Accordingly, if an employee is injured in the course of attending to personal needs, the injury is compensable. The Personal Comfort rule includes grooming, toilet breaks, rest, and refreshment needs.

[5] "An injury is accidental when either the cause or result is unexpected or accidental, although the work being done is usual or ordinary." *Zaremba v. Chrysler Corp.,* (1966) 377 Mich. 226, 139 N.W.2d 745.

[6] Refer back to *State Industrial Insurance System v. Weaver,* where a 58-year-old employee died of a heart attack shortly after completing a timed mile run required for his job retention.

Index of Cases

A

B

C

D

E

F

G

H

J

K

L

M

N

O

P

R

S

T

U

V

W

Y

Z